ESSENTIAL ENERGY BALANCING II

Essential Energy Balancing II

HEALING THE GODDESS

DIANE STEIN

THE CROSSING PRESS
BERKELEY/TORONTO

Diane Stein teaches limited women-only weekend workshops
in Florida on Essential Reiki and Essential Energy Balancing.
Contact for workshops only: dianeelk@yahoo.com

The Crossing Press
www.crossingpress.com

A Division of Ten Speed Press
PO Box 7123
Berkeley, California 94707
www.tenspeed.com

Distributed in Australia by Simon and Schuster Australia, in Canada by Ten Speed
Press Canada, in New Zealand by Southern Publishers Group, in South Africa by
Real Books, and in the United Kingdom and Europe by Airlift Book Company.

Cover and text design by Lynn Bell, Monroe Street Studios

Library of Congress Cataloging-in-Publication Data
Stein, Diane, 1948–
Essential energy balancing II : healing the goddess / Diane Stein.
        p. cm.
Includes index.
ISBN 1-58091-154-4 (pbk.)
1. Karma—Miscellanea. 2. Force and energy—Miscellanea. 3. Spiritual healing.
I. Title: Essential energy balancing two. II. Title: Essential energy balancing 2. III.
Title.
BF1045.K37S735   2003
291.2'2—dc21   2003011232

First printing, 2003
Printed in Canada

1 2 3 4 5 6 7 8 9 10 — 07 06 05 04 03

FOR BREDE

Contents

Diagrams

Acknowledgments

I would like to thank Phyllis Goozh for all the psychic work and healing we have done together in the past year. Without her understanding of Divine Director and her ability to meet his requirements for karmic release beyond the Galaxy, as well as her connection with the Shekinah, no Goddesses would be permitted to return to Earth. Her patience with me, with Divine Director, and with these seemingly endless and unforgiving processes have been beyond any and all calls of friendship or duty. I thank Na'ama Hadar also, for her work with Phyllis and me, as well as for her courage and willingness to persist with the work despite great fear and continual adversity. Of both Phyllis and Na'ama, I ask forgiveness for the phone bills, for the all nightlong workings, and for the extent of what I dragged them into for so long.

To all the rest of the thirty-six women bringing in the first groups of Goddesses, I also extend great thanks. You have followed me through years and months of difficulty without result, believing beyond belief that the results would come. I owe particular thanks to Connie Repoli, Jean Guy, Dion Tsujimura, Missy Owings, Leah Jeannesdaughter, Lynda Lichti, and Elaine Gill for their support and participation. Leah Jeannesdaughter gave me hours of channeled information just at the time it was most needed. Lynda Lichti gave me the concept of Karmic Renewal. Connie Repoli has offered healing time after time for me and for Brede.

Above all else, I thank the Goddesses, particularly my own Goddess Brede who is Earth's Great Goddess, for their willingness to return to the combat zone that is the Earth. I thank our Solar System's Great Mother Nada, our Galaxy's Light Mother Judith, and the Shekinah, our Great Cosmic Mother of All. I thank the Old One who is our planet's life force, as well. I invite the Goddesses returning to Earth now to enjoy the offerings of this planet—chocolate, shopping, jewelry, comic books, and classy clothes—and to complete the planet's healing that is their reason for being here.

I again thank Elaine Gill, Jo Ann Deck, and the people of The Crossing Press for standing by me and for publishing my books. The information of these books becomes increasingly strange in earthplane terms—but also increasingly true.

GALACTIC KARMA

When I completed the processes for *Essential Energy Balancing* (The Crossing Press, 2000) in March 1998, I thought something in my life was finished. As it turned out, however, *Essential Energy Balancing* and Earth ascension were only the beginnings of an ongoing odyssey. My 1995 start of working with the Lords of Karma developed into *We Are the Angels* (The Crossing Press, 1997) and *Essential Energy Balancing,* and it has continued in *Reliance on the Light: Psychic Protection with the Lords of Karma and the Goddess* (The Crossing Press, 2001). What I thought was a closed process still continues, and this book is the fourth in a series of at least five books on ascension and karmic healing. There will also be an *Essential Energy Balancing III* in the near future.

On May Eve (April 30) 1998, a month after I'd taught my first Essential Energy Balancing class weekend, my Goddess Brede (the Celtic Maiden Goddess Bridgh, Brigit, Bride) came to me psychically and asked, "Can I come and live with you permanently?" She has been the source of all my writing and the center of my life since she joined with me as a walk-in on June 24, 1983. A walk-in is when a higher-level aspect of a person's soul suddenly joins with her body, and some other aspects of the soul that were already in the body choose to leave, to be passed over. In answer to her invitation, I unhesitatingly said, "Yes." I asked her, "What do I have to do?" and she replied, "Make the request of the Lords of Karma." I did so and *Essential Energy Balancing II,* the processes of this book, began to be. Her coming to live with me has only been completed with the continuing work of *Essential Energy Balancing III* at Spring Equinox 2001.

In the time between, I have learned a great deal—often more than I wanted to know—about where we of Earth came from and what we have been through. I have learned a great deal too about who the Goddesses are, who we are, and what karma and ascension really mean. I was told by Brede in 1998 that Essential Energy Balancing was an ascension process, but the word had no meaning for me. I understood only that it meant clearing enough karma so that reincarnation was no longer a requirement. In New Age literature, I had read stories about people disappearing, presumably dying and "taking their bodies with them" to go to a better place. In that place, which sounded suspiciously like the Christian concept of heaven, these people would have a new existence as ascended Be-ings or even as Ascended Masters. They were not dead but only moved to a better neighborhood, so to speak, a place of Light where they would serve humanity but no longer be part of it. No mention of the Goddess was ever made.

Ascension turns out to be something very different and a great deal more complicated. If this were not the case, we would have been doing it all along and would have known much more about it. No one is going to die or disappear, with or without their bodies. Ascension is completed right here on Earth, while we are very much alive, and we will live on afterward. The place of Light is what we are on Earth to create, and the Ascended Masters who serve humanity are the ranks we may join and what we may become. Clearing Earth karma is the first step of a much more involved path, though even to accomplish this much is a great gift. With Earth ascension, the requirement for reincarnation here is completed, but we have lived and accrued karma in many places beyond Earth. We have lived thousands of lifetimes on many planets.

A brief definition of karma is in order here, as it is a concept that is (or was) a part of every religion and spirituality on Earth. While some traditions define karma in simple "eye for an eye" terms, my own understanding is much different. Karma is a concept that says that what you do comes back to you, and also says that the soul is eternal. We live many lifetimes, in a variety of places and situations, not only our current lifetime. Events and actions in every incarnation (lifetime) are accountable. All issues must be resolved, and the resolution may happen in the lifetime where the event occurred or in any subsequent life. Some sources would illustrate this with the idea that if you have been robbed in this lifetime, it is a payback for having robbed someone else in the past, in this or other lives. If you have been raped, at some time you must have been a rapist.

In my own experience of karma, issues indeed must be resolved and the resolution can occur in other lifetimes than when they originated. However, the "eye for an eye" part of karma is in question. In the years I have been working with the Lords of Karma and teaching others to work with them, it has been extremely rare to find that someone who has suffered has "deserved it," that is, that they were being paid back for their past deeds. What I have observed instead is many patterns of repeated suffering, where suffering that has not been healed repeats until healing takes place. The concept to emphasize here is the need for healing, not the need for punishment. "Eye for an eye" just doesn't apply. If a person has been robbed, she has likely been robbed in one or many of her past lives, often by the same person who has robbed her in this life. If she has been raped, she has likely been raped before, and probably by the same perpetrator.

The way, therefore, to end negative karma is not to be punished for it but to heal it. The woman who has been raped is not to blame herself for having been a rapist in some past life, as it is highly unlikely that she ever was a rapist. The more important resolution is that she heal herself of the suffering of having been raped. Doing this can be as simple as taking her rapist to court, standing up for herself and saying no to the perpetrator, seeking therapy to heal her trauma, or going to the Lords of Karma for karmic release. Understanding the karma, how and why the situation or pattern began, or even understanding that there has been a pattern or incident in one or more past lives, can be enough to release it and prevent it from returning ever again. The resolution is to heal the damage and end the suffering, not to punish or blame. Punishment does not exist in karmic healing, in which only the understanding of responsibility is relevant, and blame is a hindrance.

In every incarnation of every soul created by the Light, there is suffering. It is a fact of life. (Who and what the Light is will be discussed more fully in the chapters that follow.) Suffering is different from evil and can be a means of soul growth. It teaches compassion for others. Souls created by

3

the Light do not do evil deeds, though they can make misjudgments and do wrong deeds until they learn better. This learning is all part of a soul's growth, and part of the reason for karma. There have been evil souls, which are now destroyed, and their incarnations are being cleansed and restored to the Light, as all Be-ings were meant to be. Evil is defined as lack of love, as deliberate wrongdoing with the conscious desire to hurt, harm, or destroy other Be-ings (people, animals, or the planet). Few souls created by the Light do real evil, and none of their incarnations *are* evil. Karma is, therefore, not a method of punishment but a method of learning, healing, and soul growth.

If you have completed the work of *Essential Energy Balancing* and/or *We Are the Angels,* you have learned to work with the Lords of Karma to understand and release the suffering of your own life and past lifetimes. There is much more discussion of the concept and theory of karma in those books. As the karma of your Earth past lives has to be cleared and healed to complete Earth ascension, so does the karma of your lifetimes on other planets and galaxies need to be cleared to carry your ascension further. The way to begin this process is to work diligently to clear your Earth karma first. If you have only read the books, you have not done this work or even begun it. To clear your karma, you must examine your life and take every aspect and incident of suffering and adversity to the Lords of Karma for clearing, release, and understanding. When this is completed, or at least well underway, you may begin the work of clearing your karma from other planets and galaxies. Eventually, with *Essential Energy Balancing III,* you will clear your karma all the way through the Universe and Cosmos.

Ascension is more than clearing your karma, however. In *Essential Energy Balancing,* I described the process as having several aspects. First, you must have release and healing for all the suffering (karma) of this and other lifetimes. Second, you must be cleared and healed of all negative interference—evil, if you will—from your energy in this and all other past lives. Third, you must be reunited with the full potential of your soul's energy, and must recover your access to who you really are. This full potential means the reconnection of your DNA—to twelve or twenty-one strands in *Essential Energy Balancing,* and to your energy's full complement of DNA strands in *Essential Energy Balancing II.* This reconnection in turn gives you the ability to bring in and merge your Energy Selves (*Essential Energy Balancing*), and the possibility in *Essential Energy Balancing II* of bringing in and merging into your physical energy the energy of your Goddess.

In *Essential Energy Balancing,* you were introduced to your Higher Self, Essence Self, Goddess Self, and Goddess. If you completed the processes and worked diligently with the Lords of Karma, you merged your Higher Self, Essence Self, and Goddess Self into your physical energy, thereby increasing and raising your Light vibration considerably. For the first time, you were introduced to the idea that there is much more to you than you ever realized—more of Light, more of wisdom, more of beauty. The amount of the soul that is actually incarnated in the physical body is about as small in comparison as the size of your thumbnail. By merging and anchoring-in your Energy Selves, you considerably increased the amount of your soul that is present in your body and your daily life.

The completion of this merging is required for *Essential Energy Balancing II,* though it is possible (but not desirable) to complete the merging later. If you wish to bring in a Goddess, you must complete *Essential Energy Balancing* and all of the merging processes in sequence from that book. Until your Higher Self, Essence Self, and Goddess Self are fully merged and fused in your energy, it is not possible for your Goddess to come in or to stay with you. The completion of Earth ascension requires this merging, plus the clearing and release of at least 51 percent of your Earth karma from all lifetimes, and the clearing of at least 75 percent of all negative interference done to you on Earth.

To bring your Goddess into your energy and merge Her into you permanently requires the merging of the Energy Selves, your DNA reconnected to at least twenty-one strands, and the release of 100 percent of your Earth karma and negative interference from all Earth lifetimes. To *become* your Goddess, to fully incarnate Her into your energy, you must in addition clear 100 percent of your karma from the Galaxy (all galaxies), Universe, and Cosmos, as well as all of the negative interference done to you, your

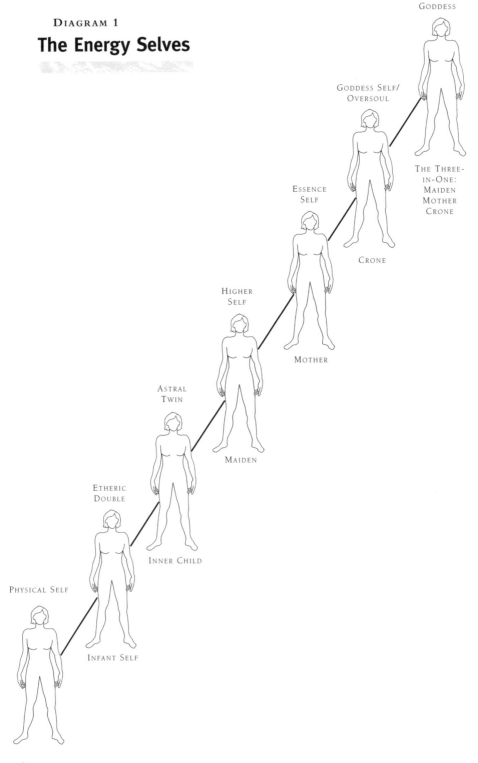

PURE LIGHT

GODDESS

DIAGRAM 1

The Energy Selves

GODDESS SELF/
OVERSOUL

THE THREE-
IN-ONE:
MAIDEN
MOTHER
CRONE

ESSENCE
SELF

CRONE

HIGHER
SELF

MOTHER

ASTRAL
TWIN

MAIDEN

ETHERIC
DOUBLE

INNER CHILD

PHYSICAL SELF

INFANT SELF

Goddess, and your core soul. You must reconnect the full complement of your DNA, which is a different amount for each individual but usually means eighty-one strands total. The processes of this book will bring you almost that far, completing your karma from this and all other galaxies you may have incarnated upon. The processes of *Essential Energy Balancing III* will complete the work, and complete your total ascension as well.

To review briefly, your Higher Self is your higher wisdom, your soul-knowing or inner guidance. She remembers everything you have learned in this lifetime and is able to help you to apply that learning. Your Essence Self is the combined wisdom of all of your Earth incarnations. She remembers all that you have learned in every Earth lifetime and thereby expands your Higher Self's learning considerably. Your Goddess Self is your Oversoul. She contains the wisdom of all the incarnations and Be-ings of your soul group, which is all the Earth lifetimes in a total of twenty-five to thirty-five people. Your Goddess is the caretaker and creator of up to thirty-five over-souls and all their incarnations. Beyond your Goddess is an entire Chain of Light and Light Be-ings, ending with your soul and the creator of all souls for this Cosmos, our Great Cosmic Mother, the Shekinah. There will be more information on all of these throughout this book.

Traditional ascension information fails to mention all that is added to who we are by the process, the growth of our Be-ings in every dimension and every way. It seems to miss the point, as the biggest bonus of all is never hinted at. Ascension means the return of the Goddess, of all the Goddesses, to the Earth and to our own daily lives. It means reconnecting with and restoring the integrity of our souls and bringing the Goddesses who are our souls' highest expressions to join with us and to "come and live with us permanently." With *Essential Energy Balancing II* and *Essential Energy Balancing III* to follow, many Goddesses will come to live and serve humanity on Earth. It will be the first time in fifteen centuries that the Goddesses can incarnate on this planet. They will do so in the energies and bodies of the women they choose to join with. Our lives will then become the source for our own healing and evolution, as well as that of the planet and the All.

While only women, and not every woman, who complete the processes of the Essential Energy Balancing series (*Essential Energy Balancing, Essential Energy Balancing II,* and *Essential Energy Balancing III*) will bring a Goddess into their energy to incarnate with them, everyone who completes these processes will benefit. Not everyone is meant to achieve ascension in this lifetime or to bring in a Goddess. We are, however, now in the new millennium and the Age of Aquarius, a long-prophesied time of planetary change and growth. The Age of Aquarius is the age of the Goddess. If you are living on Earth at this time, you are a part of the changes and have a part to play in them. You are a part of the ascension of the planet, the collective result of a critical mass of individual ascensions. Your individual healing begins the healing of the Earth and of the All.

Though everyone has a Goddess—She is a part of every Be-ing's soul—it is only women who will bring Goddesses into their energies. These essences of female divinity do not match and will not fit into male bodies. It would be like trying to fit shoes on your hands or gloves on your feet. There is nothing wrong with the shoes or gloves, they just don't belong where you are trying to put them. Men who achieve ascension will one day incarnate male divinity and male Ascended Master energies into their Be-ings, but the time for this is not now. A main thrust of planetary, Galactic, Universal, and Cosmic ascension is to restore the feminine and the Goddess to Earth and the All, to restore the balance that our very male-dominated planet, Galaxy, Universe, and Cosmos have lost. Once this balance is achieved by the return of the Goddess and many Goddesses, and by the healing of women's souls, men will begin to bring in and incarnate divine male Be-ings.

In the meantime men's job is what it has always been—to become evolved and ascended souls who are protectors of the feminine, protectors of women and the Goddess, and protectors of life and the Light. They are called upon to honor the feminine and the Goddess energy, and to clear and heal themselves of all the karma of their own incarnations on Earth and beyond. They have received as much negative interference as women have, with different emphases, and have become as disconnected from their souls and their own evolution as women have, or more so. While the negative interference done to women has been to disenfranchise and disempower them, the negative interference aimed at men has made them the agents of women's lack of power. It has also made them the perpetrators (but not the originators) of violence to women and violence in general, and this has to end. Evolved men have their jobs cut out for them—a planet, Galaxy, and beyond for them to heal. But first they must heal themselves.

Those women and men who do not complete ascension or bring in Goddesses have a role to play as well. They are laying the foundation now for ascension later, in this and other lifetimes. They are preparing the way for themselves and for the planet and beyond. The purpose of Goddesses coming back to Earth is to evolve and eventually ascend the planet and everyone on it. If your time for ascension is not now, it will come. The next steps are to evolve and complete by our Earth's ascension that of our Galaxy and all galaxies, then our Universe and all universes, our Cosmos and all cosmos' ascension—and beyond. Each Be-ing's individual growth and evolution is part of the process and the plan. Whether you bring in a Goddess or not, whether you complete your ascension at this time or not, you are a part of the Goddess's plan.

The Goddesses coming to Earth are of all ages, sizes, cultures, colors, and types. They are as varied as the women who are bringing them in. There is an infinite variety of Goddesses, and an almost infinite number. Every Earth culture has known the Goddess, and She is often described as "the Goddess of ten thousand names." All Goddesses are said to be one Goddess, but it is more accurate to say that all Goddesses (and all human and animal souls) have a common creator, the Shekinah, who is the creator Goddess of our Cosmos. Many other creator Goddesses (and male ascended Be-ings) work under Her supervision to comprise the Chain of Light. Some of the divine Be-ings coming into women's energy as Goddesses are also angels, archangels, soul archetypes, female Ascended Masters, saints, and women of herstory.

Some of the Goddesses coming to Earth are coming in threes. The Triple Goddess is traditional in many cultures, either as three aspects of one Goddess's Be-ing or three ages of one Goddess. Many of the women bringing in Goddesses have discovered that by the end of the process their Goddess is in fact three Goddesses. All of the Goddesses are ancient, but they can choose to incarnate through their women in any form, or multiple forms, that they decide to be. Some of the Goddesses are old, some are young, some are mothers, some are maidens, some are grand-mothers. The Goddesses are coming in at any and every age.

I have known for many years that my Goddess Brede is a Maiden Goddess, but when She fully joined with me I was amazed to discover that She is only fourteen years old yet full grown. She has decided to come to Earth as a child—the age seems to vary—since She has had few incarnations where She survived to grow to adulthood. She wants to grow up on Earth with me. It is not unusual for a very young woman to bring in a Crone Goddess or an older woman to bring a Maiden Goddess into her energy. Do not doubt the power of any Goddess, even if She seems to be a child.

There is also a great variety in the women that Goddesses are choosing to join with. Wiccans have always worshiped the Goddess, but to Christians She is a new idea. Yet a number of Christian women are bring-ing in Goddesses, some as saints or angels. I was concerned that these women would have difficulty in accepting the idea of bringing Goddess energy into their bodies and lives, but that has not been the case. Goddess energy is so wholly loving that all reservations fade. Women bringing in Goddesses to date have included Catholics, Protestants, Jewish women, Buddhists, Santeras, Wiccans, traditional Native Americans, and those who have no religious affiliation. Those involved with Women's Spirituality, Wicca, and the New Age have received their Goddesses with the greatest delight and probably the most understanding. The psycholo-gists among them have had the most to adjust to, but adjust they have indeed! The women come from every social class, race, and profession, from several countries, and range in age from just over twenty years old to seventy-six. They are as varied as their Goddesses.

Besides their work of ascending the planet, the Goddesses are coming to experience Earth. They share their women's sensory perceptions, seeing what the women see, feeling, hearing, tasting, and experiencing with them. New to Earth, they have a very fresh way of viewing modern life. Upon watching a loaded flatbed tow-truck pass my car while I was driving, Brede asked me in great perplexity, "Why is the car riding in a car?" Like any child, She enjoys toy stores and wants the things She sees there. The Goddesses are curious, and sometimes fearful, about being here and about what they perceive here. The sensations of Earth living take getting used to for the Goddesses, as the sensations of having them with us takes getting used to for us. The partnership is wholly delightful.

Most of the Goddesses seem to particularly like chocolate and they ask for it—they taste what their women taste. They enjoy animals, gardening, nature, jewelry, and shopping, and are especially fascinated by catalog shopping. The idea of picking things from a book to have them arrive at your door is irresistible. All Goddesses are creative and artistic, and they are delighted to help their women in artistic endeavors, as well as in the activities of everyday life. They have fears of the Earth experience, however, and their sensitive sensory abilities are far greater than ours, thus they are subject to being overwhelmed. Since they have been harmed so badly on Earth and in many other places since their originations, they can be overly cautious and afraid. A herstory of the Goddesses, and of us, is described in detail in the next chapter.

Everyone, every person and animal that is alive, has a Goddess. The process of Galactic ascension attempts to join women's Earth Be-ings with their Goddesses, bringing the Goddesses into the women's energy to join with them fully and to participate in living on Earth. When this happens, the Goddess is then made incarnate, with and in the body and physical energies of the woman She has chosen. The woman is always an incarnation of that Goddess—the Goddess she is bringing in has created her. While each of the Goddesses has created numerous women, each Goddess will choose only one woman to join permanently with, though She may speak with and do healing through many others. Thousands of women may therefore have the same Goddess, but She will choose only one to bring Her in.

The woman chosen in this way is always someone of great integrity who has dedicated herself to a life of service. She may be a metaphysical teacher, a healer, psychologist, psychic, activist, artist, or someone who works with plants, animals, or children. The woman's service may involve her job or profession, but not necessarily. Most Goddess women are teachers in the metaphysical sense, or will become so. They are evolved metaphysically, or the Goddess they bring in will evolve and teach them. The Goddesses come here to heal and to teach, and those women who bring in Goddesses will aid others to bring in Goddesses as well. Women are chosen for the ability of their Goddess to work through them to do the things that particular Goddess wishes to do. To be chosen by a Goddess in this way is a great honor.

If you wish to be chosen to bring in a Goddess, it is both a joy and a responsibility. Your end of the bargain is to be the best that you can be as a person, to grow and evolve in every way possible, and to work actively at it. It is essential to do the work of clearing, healing, and facing your karma, and to work with the Lords of Karma intensively to do so. You must have a commitment to your total healing and the persistence to follow it through, even when the going gets difficult. You must be willing to evolve, and must have the drive and desire for ascension and for the joining. You must have the willingness to share your life with a divine Be-ing, one who will give you great love but who will require your attention and your care. I once asked Brede why She had chosen me, and Her reply was, "Because you longed for me." And I did.

Much of how far you go in this depends on your willingness to face yourself and to do some intensive karmic work. Only those who do this will bring in their Goddess, and only those who persevere to the end will be granted ascension. The processes are not always easy, but the hard work required brings results that are well worth the effort. If you do the work, all the help you need will be there for you. There will be major transformations of your energy and your life along the way. Some of the changes may not seem pleasant, and they can also be very scary, but they are necessary. You will be forced to look at things in your life and herstory, and that of your Goddess, that are not pleasant to know about or to face. Some of what we have experienced has been horrible, and our Goddesses have suffered even more than we have. To bring in your Goddess, you will be required to heal Her and to heal yourself, and to do the work of protecting and clearing both of you from negative interference and from evil.

Negative interference is a concept that was discussed in *Essential Energy Balancing*. Evil is a subject that many metaphysical people refuse to look at or to face in themselves or in the world. When I have discussed this in my workshops, the women I teach frequently argue with me about it, or even walk out of the classes. They tell me that there is no negative energy, only Light. They tell me that the things I call evil are only in our imaginations and if we ignore them they go away. They say that by discussing wrong and evil, I give it power. They tell me to just use "white light," and they tell me I am wrong. Process IX in *Essential Energy Balancing* is a process of clearing yourself of negative interference from Earth. I tell the doubters to bear with me until they go through this process. By the time they do so, they see enough of evil clearing and leaving their own energies that they begin to believe.

To do the work of *Essential Energy Balancing II,* you must believe in negative interference, or at least be willing to take my word for it until you have perceptions of your own. A great part of *Essential Energy Balancing II* is involved in clearing and protecting yourself and your Goddess from negative interference and evil. I do not use the term "evil" indiscriminately, as you will see in the next chapter. We have been subjected to great evil, not only on Earth but on every planet we have lived since our origins. Our origins were blighted and actually destroyed by the first beginnings of evil and hate, as were the places we fled to for safety. The Goddesses have been targeted for destruction by evil since their souls' creations. To bring a Goddess in, you must clear your energies and Hers of the harm that has been done, and remove all access of evil from Her and from you. If you are not bringing in a Goddess, it is vital to clear yourself, and essential if you wish to attain Galactic ascension or beyond.

It is important to state here, if it is not clear already, that the evil we are speaking of was almost always done *to* you, rather than *by* you. There have been many evil souls, who created evil incarnations, but these have now been destroyed. If you are on the ascension path and have come far enough in working with the Light to be drawn to this book and to choose to work with it, you are most certainly not an evil soul. If you are the creation of evil, you will *be* evil and this work will not interest you; you will probably never even be aware of it. If you are of an evil soul and come to this work, you will be denied power but granted cleansing and healing to return you to the Light. None of this is likely, however. You may be assured that you are a creation of the Light and are welcomed by it. You are a Be-ing on the ascension path.

In the first *Essential Energy Balancing* processes, you were asked to raise the ability of your energy to hold Light by reconnecting your DNA. You were asked to clear yourself of the negative interference that has followed you through all your Earth lifetimes. You were also asked to reconnect with your Energy Selves and your Goddess. In these new processes of *Essential Energy Balancing II,* you will ask to do similar things, but on a higher and much more intensive level. You have completed your work with Earth karma, or come a long way toward completing it, and now it is time to clear your karma from beyond Earth, from you and your Goddess's incarnations on other planets in the Galaxy. If the clearings were intense for Earth, they will be much more so beyond it. They will become more intense yet if you bring in a Goddess, as you will undertake the clearing of both your karma and Hers. If you continue through *Essential Energy Balancing III,* the processes and clearings will increase even more in both intensity and complexity.

If the work is more difficult, however, the rewards are also greater. You are reaching for the Brass Ring, for the joy of being everything you were meant to be, and for possibly having a Goddess "come and live with you permanently" besides. By clearing yourself from evil, you make way for the full manifesting of the Light in your energy and soul. You are working to restore your energy and soul to the Creational Birthright of the Light you were created to have and to be. You will become much more the person of Light that you truly are, and every aspect of your life will reflect the changes in positive ways.

You will also have an opportunity to heal more of the circumstances that remain difficult and unfinished in your daily life. If something wrong in your life has not changed with your Lords of Karma work and the release of Earth karma, the chances are good that the source of the problem originated in Galactic incarnations. It may have even originated in your incarnations beyond the Galaxy, in the Universe or Cosmos. On a number of occasions, I have been granted requests by the Lords of Karma but nothing seemed to change. These were just the issues that responded to Galactic Karma and to working with Divine Director, the keeper of karma for the Galaxy and Universe. This is another chance to heal your life and to make it what you wish it to be. If you have done your work conscientiously with the Lords of Karma, the issues that still remain are not from Earth. *Essential Energy Balancing II* is the opportunity to clear, release, and heal karmas that have seemed impossible to resolve until now.

While in *Essential Energy Balancing* you made your requests for karmic clearing to your own group of the Lords of Karma, in *Essential Energy Balancing II* you will meet a new level of ascended Be-ings. Our Great Mother Nada is the keeper and final decider and arbiter of karma from our Earth and Solar System. At times, your Lords of Karma group appealed to Her for decisions regarding your requests, and you may have met Her in your work with them. The presiding Mother of our Galaxy, called Light Mother, is kept very protected in Her purity and is far less approachable than Nada. Her representative in all requests, and who you will address in clearing Galactic Karma and karma of the Universe and Cosmos, is Divine Director. He is a member of the Galactic, Universal, and Cosmic Karmic Boards, and is Light Mother's liaison to our Earth and Solar System. Nada may be present for your requests as well, as the healing of your Galactic Karma affects the Solar System and Earth.

Divine Director is a title, it is not his name; he has had incarnations on Earth but not recently, and his approach is very mental in nature. You will address him for all requests. The Light Mother for our Galaxy is named Judith. She is very innocent and has little comprehension of the sufferings of people in bodies. She told me once that She heals planets, and sometimes Goddesses, but not people. Light Mother has created only one incarnation for Earth, that of Mother Mary. If you see Her in healing, you will be aware of the blue color that is often associated with the Mother of Jesus. Her presence at any time is a great gift. There is a Light Mother for each galaxy. It should go without saying that these Be-ings are to be addressed only with the greatest respect.

Clearing Galactic Karma and beyond also involves, on a variety of levels, the Light Mothers' Galactic Creational Computers or Mind Grids. These computers must be programmed, or reprogrammed, by your requests to change your karma for the Galaxy and beyond. Your request must be granted by Divine Director, and made in the proper and acceptable format and wording for the reprogramming to take place. The means for changing the Creational Computers, your Galactic Akashic Records, is in the vibration of the words of your requests, and these wordings are much more complex and demanding than they were in working with the Lords of Karma.

The processes of *Essential Energy Balancing II* are very precise, and often frustratingly long, but they must be done exactly as written to gain the results you are asking for. With a slip in your wording or your process, the response from Divine Director will be no. The processes and formats get somewhat easier in *Essential Energy Balancing III* for releasing your karma from the Universe and Cosmos. In *Essential Energy Balancing III,* where the requests must be granted by Divine Director and the Shekinah together, Nada has agreed to intervene and help us. The words and formats are therefore less complex and less involved.

The process of clearing Galactic Karma is also the process of restoring the balance of Universal Law and ethics and of ending duality in your energy and on Earth. We have been told frequently that everywhere there is Light there must be its opposite, that all things come in pairs, in Yin and Yang. This is the way that it has been but not the way it was supposed to be. You will understand this more clearly in the next chapter. The work of *Essential Energy Balancing II* and later of *Essential Energy Balancing III* is designed to end what is evil and negative in duality forever. Opposites are said to be divine, but most are not.

In a final comment for this introduction, I would like to state that it is the Goddesses themselves who pick the women they will incarnate through. If you are a woman and wish to bring in a Goddess, you may ask Divine Director and the Lords of Karma for the privilege, and they will grant it or not. You may not demand it or specify which Goddess is to come. No one other than the Goddesses and the Karmic Board (of which Divine Director is a part) can make the choice. I have had women in my workshops insist that they wanted a particular Goddess to come into them, and they have been angry with me when it didn't happen. I have no say in the matter, and you have no say in the matter either. The granting of a Goddess is the greatest of gifts from the Light. It is something that is bestowed, not demanded.

WHERE WE CAME FROM

Humanity did not originate or evolve on Earth, and we were not created here. We were created in another cosmos by our Great Cosmic Mother, the Shekinah, as Be-ings and souls of the greatest Light. It is said that the Shekinah created Herself of the raw materials of life—of Light, sound, vibration, frequency, and energy. This may indeed be so, or She may have been created in turn by Be-ings beyond our current knowing. Our understanding at this time can only begin in our original cosmos, on the unnamed planet of our first origin, but this beginning of who we are will be enough for our purposes now. Suffice it to say that the Shekinah was the first Goddess and the first creator of all the souls and Goddesses that followed.

The Shekinah's first creation was Her Consort, the first male Be-ing of Light, the first God. Traditional Old Testament information has reversed the process, stating that God created the Shekinah to be His wife and helper, but this is not so. The Shekinah created Her mate, and we have given Him the name of God or YHWH or Jehovah. He was the warrior and protector of life, and the Shekinah was life's creator. From this point, all the Be-ings/souls/Goddesses created by the Shekinah were made in pairs. The DNA to perpetuate this pairing was installed in the replication of all Be-ing, programmed into the creational Mind Grids of the Cosmos. These Mind Grids are also the Cosmic Creational Computers or Akashic Records of all Be-ings and Be-ing. With the creation of each Goddess thereafter, Her Twin Flame was created simultaneously for Her companionship, protection, and delight.

The Shekinah's next creation was Her daughter, the Goddess Na'ama, whose name means "Beauty." Na'ama was indeed a Goddess of great beauty, and a creator Goddess of the highest Light as well. Na'ama was created as the first Great Mother, with the job of making a sun and solar system to support life—there had been only deep space until then. To aid Na'ama in Her job, Her first creations for Her solar system were Na'ama's own daughters, the Goddesses Cybele, Lilith, Aleya, and Persephone. As the first Light Mother, Persephone created a galaxy to surround and support Na'ama's solar system. With Persephone's galaxy and Na'ama's solar system in place, a planet within the solar system was made by Aleya, the first Great Goddess. The life force of that planet, embodied in a Be-ing we call a dragon, was created by Cybele. When the planet and its life force were ready, the life forms of that planet were created by Lilith, who was to be the planetary Earth Mother.

Each of these Goddesses had a Twin Flame created with Her, and though they were created in the highest Light, they began to be discontent. They watched their partner Goddesses create, and they wanted to create as well. They wanted the power and the control of life, and their desire resulted in destruction, devastation, and death. In their attempts to take creational power, they captured some of the Shekinah's substance of life—the DNA of creation—and mutated it, trying to bend these energies to their own will. The result was something they could not control. It caused a poison that destroyed life instead of fostering it, creating the mutation for duality and evil. The first life that was mutated was their own.

They next used these mutated energies on the Goddess Cybele and the planetary life force dragon She had formed. Cybele and Her dragon were poisoned, attacked, tortured, betrayed, torn apart, and almost destroyed. This was done deliberately in the understanding that if they survived, the dragon life force would destroy the mutations and with them the Twin Flames' (now Evil Twins) newfound power. The poisoning of the life force resulted in the near death of Cybele and the mutation of the dragon Herself. The dragon then replicated to create its own Evil Twin duplicate. Because the dragon was the life force, all life was then affected, and the

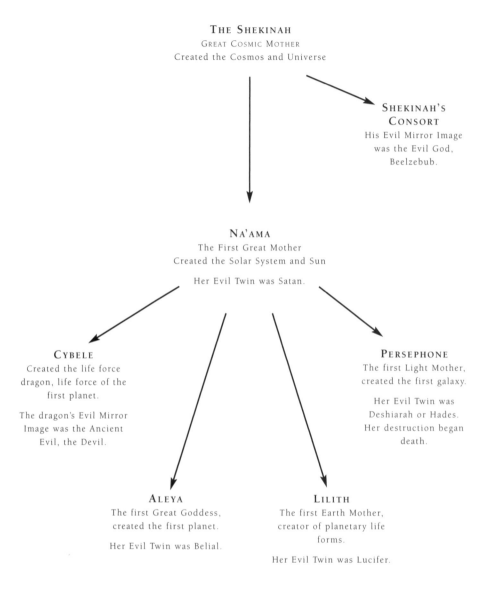

DIAGRAM 2

The Origins of Our Creation

THE SHEKINAH
GREAT COSMIC MOTHER
Created the Cosmos and Universe

**SHEKINAH'S
CONSORT**
His Evil Mirror Image
was the Evil God,
Beelzebub.

NA'AMA
The First Great Mother
Created the Solar System and Sun

Her Evil Twin was Satan.

CYBELE
Created the life force
dragon, life force of the
first planet.

The dragon's Evil Mirror
Image was the Ancient
Evil, the Devil.

PERSEPHONE
The first Light Mother,
created the first galaxy.

Her Evil Twin was
Deshiarah or Hades.
Her destruction began
death.

ALEYA
The first Great Goddess,
created the first planet.

Her Evil Twin was Belial.

LILITH
The first Earth Mother,
creator of planetary life
forms.

Her Evil Twin was Lucifer.

Creational Computers for that planet, solar system, and galaxy—connected to and anchored in the dragon—now contained the mutation. All planetary life force dragons to come would now be created with the mutation for evil duplicates.

From this point, all of life and all the Goddesses' Twin Flames who were thereafter created carried the poisonous and deadly change. Instead of Twin Flames, with each creation of a new Goddess's soul was created a Be-ing of evil, an Evil Twin with the programming and intent to destroy Her. With the creation of each planet, solar system, and galaxy, each life form and each individual life, an Evil Twin was also generated.

The first Twin Flames to become Evil Twins were the original discontents. These were the Twin Flames of the Goddesses Na'ama, Lilith, Aleya, and Persephone. The now-Evil Twin of Na'ama is known to us today as Satan, whose name in Hebrew means "adversary" and "the first to sin." Lilith's Evil Twin was Lucifer or Sammael, "he who betrayed the Light." Aleya's was Belial, who was known as "hell's ambassador," and Persephone's was known as Deshiarah or Hades to the ancient Greeks.

The Consort of the Shekinah was attacked in the same way that Cybele's dragon was attacked, to create a mirror image evil duplicate, an Evil God that we know today as Beelzebub, Lord of Chaos. The Consort Himself was taken captive by the Evil Twins.

The Evil Mirror Image of the life force dragon, the mutation that caused the creation of evil with every creation of the Light, is known to us as the Ancient Evil, or the Devil. These are all Old Testament Earth names and may have not been their real names, but they are the last remembrances of them that we have among the distortions of space and time. They were also known as the Fallen Angels.

The Evil Twins attacked the Goddesses they were created to protect, and the attacks resulted in the placing of the mutations of duality in each. The mutations in the Goddess Na'ama caused Her to create demons (again, a subjective Earth term) that were perversions of the life force dragon and modeled after them. These resembled lizards and were known as such, as were the evil replications of the life force dragon and the replications of the Evil Twins. What evil created had the appearance of lizards and the DNA to replicate and perpetuate them. Instead of the populating of the Goddesses' planets and galaxies with a myriad of life forms of the Light, they were populated by lizards/demons instead—each with the intent for destruction and harm.

These mutations in Na'ama subverted and perverted Her ability to create the Light and to be the Light. Remember, She was the Great Mother of a solar system. They prevented Her from being connected to the Light and the positive creational life force. Her Soul Matrix was broken open by Satan so the demons She created could destroy Her. The destruction moved up and down through the chain of creation—upward to the Shekinah and Her Consort, horizontally to other Goddesses, and multiplied downward through Her daughters and all of life. What was done to Her was also done to Her twin sister Lilith, the Earth Mother of the living planet in Na'ama's solar system, and to the planet's Great Goddess Aleya.

These actions constituted Original Sin, though the story has come to Earth in a far different and much distorted form. Na'ama and Her better known twin/creation Lilith are credited as evil Be-ings who birthed monsters, killed babies, seduced men, brought dis-eases, and wreaked havoc on Earth. In fact, these Goddesses were the creators of much of life, and it is their Evil Twins who have done the horrors attributed to them. This pattern of Goddesses being blamed and continually cursed for what was done by their evil counterparts has been repeated again and again. The dragons created as the life force of each planet have been branded evil as well, named Leviathan and (mistakenly) Satan, and killed triumphantly in the legends of every ancient hero. The labeling of our creator Goddesses as evil has extended to all women, as has the institutionalized cursing of women and all Goddesses. Na'ama and Lilith are daily and unjustly cursed in Judaism to this day.

The story of Demeter and Persephone that we know from Greek mythology (herstory) began in our original galaxy too. Persephone was attacked in much the same way that Cybele, Na'ama, Lilith, and Aleya were attacked, and with much the same results. She was a very young and very innocent Maiden Goddess at the time, probably only ten or eleven years old. A Light Mother is a pure Be-ing, and this one was not only fouled and mutated, but Her soul was destroyed. She was abducted and raped by Her Evil Twin Deshiarah, who was also known on Earth as Hades. Her Soul Matrix was shattered, and She was separated from the Light. Many souls of Goddesses died at that time. (They are now being resurrected by the Shekinah.) The Soul Matrix mutations that Persephone suffered caused the creational beginnings of all death, as all the life forms of Her galaxy were then cut short, blighted, fouled, tainted by evil, and ended—as Hers had been. Persephone indeed became the ruler of the underworld, of the dead and of dead souls.

The Shekinah and all the other Goddesses whose souls were still alive fled their cosmos, along with the Twin Flames who had not turned evil. These earliest Goddesses included Athena, Rhea, Isis, Aiyesha, Kwan Yin, Judith, Parvati, and Kali Ma. Their uncorrupted consorts included Tion (Athena's Twin Flame), St. Germaine (Aiyesha's), Melchizadek, and Divine Director (whose Twin Flames had been destroyed), El Morya (whose Twin Flame is our Great Mother Nada), Sanat Kumara (Parvati's Twin Flame), and Kuthumi (Kwan Yin's Twin Flame). The Goddesses brought with them the means to recreate the life forms that were lost, and Lilith's animals had not been mutated to create duality. They traveled in a spaceship piloted by Tion, left their planet, solar system, and galaxy, and traveled even beyond their original universe and cosmos. They settled on a planet in the Andromeda star system, in our Cosmos, in the Pleiades.

After they fled, without the Shekinah's and the other Goddesses' Light and with the mutation of the solar system's life force dragon, the energies the Evil Twins had stolen went completely out of control. They escalated into a thermonuclear fusion holocaust that destabilized and destroyed their entire system. The planet, solar system, and galaxy were destroyed, while the universe and cosmos, turned evil, were not. All that remained of the solar system was its burnt-out sun, left as a black hole in space. The Evil Twins and the Evil Mirror Images they had created remained, including that of the mutated planetary dragon, and they continued to multiply and create evil, in a perversion of the creational abilities of the Shekinah, the Goddesses, and the Light. Eventually they followed the Goddesses to their new home.

Tion's Creator Light Ship, and the fleet of other Light Ships that he and other Twin Flames had built, was put as a sentinel around the Goddesses' planet. The ships housed the Twin Flames and some of the Goddesses, who also technologically sealed the new Cosmos against incursion by the evils of the old. This was successful only for a while. The Evil Twin of the destroyed Light Mother Persephone was sent to break the seal. Deshiarah succeeded, slipping past the sentinels to insert the mutation for duality into the Mind Grid Creational Computers of the new Cosmos. He attacked and damaged another Light Mother who tried to stop him. From there the programming for evil and devastation spread downward through the new universe, through the galaxies within that universe, and through the solar systems and planets within each galaxy.

As the Goddesses began to create and recreate the Light, Evil Twins were once again formed, and those who were already formed came to the Goddesses' new planet to destroy them. With all things created in duality, Tion's protecting Creator Light Ship was followed by an Evil Creator Ship. Newly created planetary dragons carried the mutation of duality with them to all planets and the life force of all planets, to multiply the mutations through all of life. The now-evil remains of our original cosmos were brought to encase and wrap around our current Cosmos. Our Cosmos of the Light was surrounded and permeated by destruction and devastation.

On their planet in the Pleiades, the Goddesses had a short period of peace. They built a civilization of temples of the Light, learning centers of healing, art, architecture, and beauty. These temples became the universities of the Cosmos, and students came from inhabited planets everywhere to learn at them. Each Goddess was in charge of Her own temple of learning. The Goddesses also began to create daughter Be-ings, other Goddesses, and most of the Goddesses we know today were created there. When it became clear that each Goddess created also generated an Evil Twin, the Goddesses experimented in generating soul aspects of

DIAGRAM 3
Where We Came From

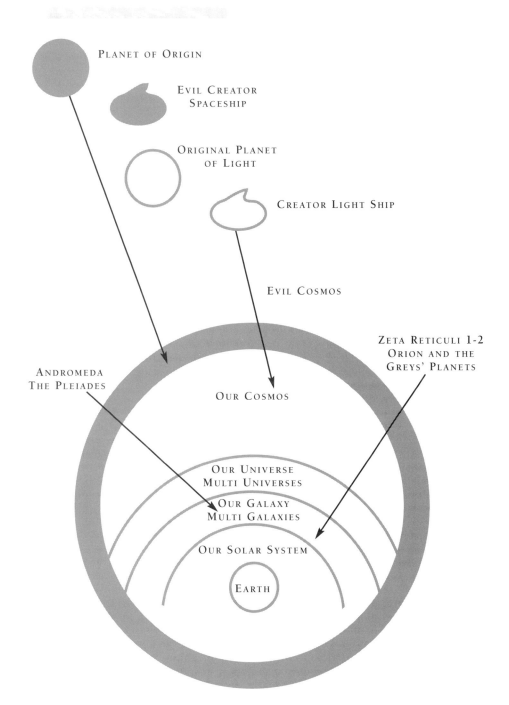

PLANET OF ORIGIN

EVIL CREATOR
SPACESHIP

ORIGINAL PLANET
OF LIGHT

CREATOR LIGHT SHIP

EVIL COSMOS

ZETA RETICULI 1-2
ORION AND THE
GREYS' PLANETS

ANDROMEDA
THE PLEIADES

OUR COSMOS

OUR UNIVERSE
MULTI UNIVERSES

OUR GALAXY
MULTI GALAXIES

OUR SOLAR SYSTEM

EARTH

themselves at a Light level too low to activate the evil mutations. This is where people, especially the women who are bringing in Goddesses now, were first formed. It is also where all humanity was separated from the Goddess. The solution was considered temporary, with the process of ascension the means of reuniting the aspects with their creators.

After the new Cosmos, our Cosmos, was breached and the Creational Computers reprogrammed to activate mutation, the Goddesses were forced to stop creating. Everything they made, whether planet or person, contained the soul mutation that carried its own destruction. They sought the means to end these mutations, but none was found. The Evil Creator Ship brought a full invasion from their original cosmos. The Ancient Evil (Devil) arrived, and with him all the Evil Twins, and the lizard Be-ings cloned by the mutated dragon. These had the ability to appear as Be-ings of Light, the ability to shift their molecular structures to look as they wished to appear. The younger and newer of the Goddesses and women had not seen these Be-ings before, and they were deceived by them. Even the more experienced Goddesses did not recognize them at first; they did not yet know that the sealing of the Cosmos had been breached.

The Evil Twins built their own temples, the first satanic temple proto-types. They were portals of evil, energetically connected through the black hole that remained of their sun, and tied into the remains of the now-evil cosmos that the Goddesses had fled. The energy source of these temples was the mutated dragon and the nuclear fusion holocaust energies. These energies had the ability to poison all of life. The purpose of these temples, and of their presence on the planet, was what it had always been—to destroy the Goddesses and all their creations, to destroy the Light.

The women the Goddesses had created were less powerful and more vulnerable, and their Be-ings offered access to the Goddesses they were incarnated from. The Evil Twins, masked as Light Be-ings, first enticed one very young woman into their temple where she was drugged, repeatedly raped, and put under satanic control. Through her, her Goddess was also attacked, much damaged, and marked for tracking and continued harm by Evil Be-ings. Both Goddess and woman were "negatively sealed," their energy tapped into to insert evil control by those in the rituals. Once they had access, the Evil Twins could use the Goddess's Light to harm Her and others, and the access would incarnate and reincarnate through every subsequent lifetime. A piece of the soul essence of both Goddess and woman was taken by the Evil Twins, held by them to complete their control. Other women and their Goddesses were attacked and negatively sealed in the same ways, either duped, drugged, or abducted for the sealing and markings to be inserted in their energies and their DNA.

The Evil Twins and their cohorts fueled their wrongs with the powerful use of curses, spells, ritual abuse, chants, negative symbols, hexes, incantations, and enchantments. This was the origin of such interference, and it completed the establishment of the Chain of Evil, beginning here with the Ancient Evil. They also fueled their workings with the perverted creational energies they had stolen from the Shekinah and the other creation Goddesses, and with the poisons of the nuclear fusion holocaust. They used all of these on the Goddesses and their women in the Pleiades. One by one all the temples of Light were taken over by evil. Eventually all the Goddesses and women were poisoned en masse, using the fusion holocaust energies to contaminate their souls and their Be-ings. These poisonings added to the Soul Matrix damage and mutations from their original planet, compounding them and compounding the spread of evil. The women were dying of these lethal energies, and the Goddesses were much damaged by them, when Tion and the Creator Light Ship removed them from their planet to flee again to a new home.

One of the women now bringing in a Goddess has a memory of Tion leaving her on their newest planet, and of her sadness at being left. There was nothing else to be done, however, but to flee and apparently little choice of where to go. The women and Goddesses incarnated this time on a pair of planetary systems that were already inhabited. One was a planet in the Orion star system, and the other was three planets in a system nearby. I will call one Orion and the other the Greys' planets, as I have no clearer names for them. The Greys' star system may be Zeta Reticula. Some of the women and Goddesses went to Orion, some to the Greys' planets,

DIAGRAM 4

The Chain of Evil and Duality

THE COSMOS	Source Planet from Beyond the Evil Cosmos EVIL COSMOS EVIL CREATOR SPACESHIP THE ANCIENT EVIL (Evil Twin of the Shekinah) All Evil Sorcery, Conjures, Spells, Rituals, Poisoning, Androids
THE UNIVERSE	THE EVIL GOD (Evil Twin of the Shekinah's Consort) EVIL TWINS OF THE ELOHIM (Lucifer, Satan) MOTHER BODIES (All Replication of Evil)
THE GALAXY	MUTATED PLANETS THE EVIL GREYS ORION THE EVIL HYBRIDS EVIL TWIN COMPUTERS Cosmos Breached Evil Encodings Placed in the Light and Galactic Creation EVIL TWINS OF THE LIGHT MOTHERS (Fallen Archangels) THE MASTERMIND (Evil Twin of St. Germaine) (Fail-Safes, Booby Traps, and Mechanisms)
EARTH AND SOLAR SYSTEM	THE CARTEL (Evil Twins of the Karmic Board) THE CONGLOMERATE (Evil Twins of the Lords of Karma) EVIL CLANS EVIL TWINS OF THE GODDESSES (Fallen Archangels) EARTH EVIL TWIN OF EARTH DRAGON

and some incarnated eventually in both places. The Greys' planets were the place that Tion and Athena had chosen for their home, and they were the creator God and Goddess there, equivalent to the Shekinah in our original cosmos.

Again we were followed and persecuted, and as in the Pleiades the original evils were compounded. Orion was taken over fully and very quickly. It became a place of genetic manipulation and hybridization, of advanced technologies of destruction and persecution, of conjured evils, of sadism and torture. The original mutated dragon's cloned lizards became hybridized here, mixed with the genetics of the mutated-to-evil Orion life force dragon. Beelzebub ruled Orion and oversaw the creation of powerful Evil Hybrids who incarnated their genetics into people of ill will—a parody of the Goddesses' incarnation of men and women. These were the Evil Clans, and they had the ability to activate the negative sealing done to the Goddesses and women in the Pleiades. They were created and programmed to destroy the Goddesses and their women, and all of the Light.

Human-animal hybrids were also created on Orion, along with clones (some in human-animal form) of the Goddesses, Goddess women, and men, using the pieces of soul essence taken from them in the evil temples. Satanic temples were also recreated on Orion, still connected through the black hole to the Evil Cosmos. Orion was the source of the Evil Eye, and of the manifestations of bugs, spiders, snakes, lizards, and other creepy things often seen in the clearing of people's energies. Some of these were embryos placed in our gene makeup to manifest from one incarnation to another. Some were holograms, projections of images that were used to draw our attention while greater harm was done elsewhere. Mother Bodies were created on Orion, mechanical hives for the rapid generation of mutated life forms in the Universe. The genetics of all of this was put into us on Orion after the takeover of Evil and the destruction of the Light on that planet.

All of these, and a clone of the Orion mutated dragon, were eventually perpetrated upon the Earth. Orion was the source of other damages placed in women's and Goddesses' creational energies, in all people, plants, and animals, in all of life, and eventually in our Earth and Solar System's Creational Computers. We were imprinted on Orion with fear, and this fear was used as a marking to track and torment us. They used advanced technologies and placed them to reincarnate in our energies. There were transistors, implants, holograms, tractor beams of destabilizing and electrocuting energies, systems of wiring, black box transformers, and other magnetic and electrical-type circuitry and mechanisms. They had spaceships and weaponry of mass destruction, mechanical rather than nuclear in type. Orion became a place of suffering very quickly for those who migrated there, and we carried too much of Orion with us when we left.

The Greys' planets were also taken over by Orion and those who invaded Orion, but the Greys' planets put up a fight that has lasted thousands of years. Though three-quarters of the population and planets were fully taken over, Tion and his forces continued to fight, and his planets have now been reclaimed. Lucifer, Satan, and Belial ruled the opposition on the three planets of the Greys. They brought with them the fusion energies of the original destruction of our source planet and hybridized those energies. They mixed Orion DNA with Greys' and other DNA, and mixed and adapted technologies from all the planets they had taken over. They had weaponry of mass destruction, nuclear fission and fusion energy, and hyperspace technology and spaceships.

The Chain of Evil added a new link with the Greys' planets, as the evil duality that was multiplying through the Cosmos produced Evil Twins of the Lords of Karma, St. Germaine, and the members of the Karmic Board. I have named these the Mastermind (St. Germaine's Evil Mirror), the Conglomerate (Evil Mirror Images of the Lords of Karma), and the Cartel (Evil Twins of the Karmic Boards). These were highly opportunistic forces to add to the mix. They were evil Be-ings of great power and cunning, and they originated on the Greys' planets. The manipulation of the Creational Computers caused evil duplicates of every type, including of the Light Mothers' computers themselves, and of all the Chain of Light. After the Orion takeover, the Greys' ability to reproduce was mutated and reduced.

The many flying saucer abductions of people from Earth for sexual and genetic sampling were done by mutated evil Greys who were seeking to regain control of their reproduction.

Long before things got this bad, the Goddesses had already created Earth and were planning to leave the Greys' planets. Their Light had been much reduced by this time, with an accumulation of attacks from their original planet and from the Pleiades, Orion, and the negative Greys. The combined forces of Orion and the evil Greys had met Tion and the forces of the Light in many desperate battles, but evil was still winning. Tion and his Light Ships brought the Goddesses and Goddess people to Earth, but again evil followed us to the new planet. Our heritage from the combination of Orion and evil Grey attacks was layers of weaponry placed in our Solar System and planet to destroy them. These mechanisms looked like black bars, and they planted the seeds of environmental destruction, disease, and the perpetuation of duality. Everything created by the Light on Earth would still create a twin of evil.

The women and their Goddesses were a primary target of these attacks. To assure the separation of the women from their Goddesses, mechanisms to create altering frequencies were developed so that the Goddesses' energies would no longer match their women's. Weaponry of destruction was placed in the creations of the Goddess unions, set to detonate if the Goddesses and women rejoined. There were fail-safes and booby traps, triggers, trip mechanisms, and destruction blueprints of every type. From the time of the women's creations in the Pleiades, the plan had been to reunite them with their Goddesses and raise their energies back to ascension (Goddess rejoined) levels as soon as the way could be found to stop the creation of evil duality. When the Goddesses and women came to Earth, these plans were further complicated.

Our early incarnations on Earth brought the manifestation and activation of these weapons and plans, and still more attacks upon the Goddesses, their women, and the Goddess unions, as well as attacks upon life on Earth itself. There were three representative key lifetimes, those of Mu, Atlantis, and the time of King Arthur. By the end of these, the

Goddesses had been driven from the Earth and separated wholly from the women they incarnated and with whom they were meant to rejoin.

Mu was our first civilization on Earth. The Goddesses and women incarnated there and created an underground culture in caves that was much like what had been lost in the Pleiades. There were temples of Light and higher learning, and an aura of excitement and great innocence. That innocence was ended, however, by a combined Orion and evil Grey invasion at a time when the women appeared above ground. A mass slaughter of the women resulted, with the Goddesses taken over by Orion technology. They were effectively "killed," wired with negative circuitry, and then reactivated almost as robots for a short but traumatic time. The Light Ships over Mu were powerless to stop it, and a ship of Tion's fighters was lost in the attempt.

While this was happening on the ground, all the levels of creation were simultaneously attacked to destroy the blueprints of the Galactic Cord systems, the means by which the Goddesses and women could rejoin. Components of these systems can be regenerated, but not if the blueprints are gone. The programmings were removed from the Creational Computers, not only of the Earth but also of our Solar System, Galaxy, Universe, and Cosmos. The experiment of Mu ended there. Grey weaponry also destabilized the Planetary Grids in an attempt to mutate the Earth's life force dragon. This in turn caused the massive earthquakes that destroyed the entire civilization. It was done by alien technology, not by people of Earth. It was one more battle and one more loss in a very long and tragic war.

Atlantis was another key civilization on Earth. In this case, the interference of the Evil Twins and entire Chain of Evil were combined with Orion and negative Grey technology. The culture was coopted and cannibalized, and eventually the same Be-ings and energies that destroyed Mu, the Pleiades, and our planet of origin destroyed Atlantis. As in the Pleiades, people were once again deceived as to the intent of the other-planet Be-ings who entered there, and they finally took Atlantis over. The destruction was not done by Earth people but by evil alien conquest. As was done on Mu, the technologies involved vibrating the crystal matrix of the planet with frequencies that caused it to destabilize. We came just short of planetary destruction at that time.

Many or all of the women now bringing in Goddesses were also on Atlantis. The Goddesses themselves were not present, having been effectively separated from the women they incarnated by the events of Mu. Remember, however, that the women were created by their Goddesses as stepped-down versions of themselves. The human-animal hybrids of Orion were present on Atlantis, as well as a variety of other corrupt technologies. The end result for the women and Goddesses was further hybridization of human DNA, further mutation of it and of the abilities of women to achieve ascension, reunion, and rejoining with their Goddesses. Atlantis was destroyed by Orion-Grey technologies ruled by the Chain of Evil. Some of the alteration of frequencies was permanent, further preventing the women and Goddesses from rejoining.

Next came the time of King Arthur and a Saxon lifetime just preceding Arthur's birth. A combined Orion and evil Greys' attack on the planet resulted in a clone of the mutated Orion dragon being placed in Solar System creation and in the Earth itself. This event has been described in legend as the terrifying fight between two dragons in the sky on the night that King Arthur was conceived. The second dragon was our planet's life force dragon of the Light. As the clone entered the atmosphere, Light Ships of every type attempted to defeat it and prevent its coming to Earth. They were only partially successful. The Orion dragon fell into the Atlantic Ocean and remained dormant there, waiting for orders to activate. It was created as the Evil Twin of our planetary life force.

In Saxon country nearby and at the same time, a group of priestesses was holding ritual. Each was paired by a man, who stood behind her, and the ritual was being led by a woman controlled by a priest. The intent of the ritual was to force the Goddesses to leave the planet once and for all, in the guise of protecting them from evil. The women were all incarnations of Goddesses, and they had reluctantly agreed or been coerced into agreeing to the plan. The excuse was that the Goddesses couldn't be protected and therefore should be kept away for their own safety. There was an alien agenda here, of course. As soon as the ritual was completed, each man partnering a woman killed her. In this ritual, the planetary frequencies were again altered so the Goddesses not only couldn't rejoin their women, but also couldn't tolerate being in the vibrations. With the dragon clone, the results awaited activation.

Next was the time of King Arthur himself. Every woman bringing in a Goddess has memories of this time, of either incarnating as a Priestess of Avalon or a member of the Round Table or court. The lifetime was considered so crucial that Archangel Michael himself was incarnated as Sir Lancelot, and Twin Flame and Karmic Board member El Morya was incarnated as Arthur's adviser, Merlin. This was one last attempt for Right to prevail over Might, and it almost succeeded. The Evil Hybrid fueled plots of Morgause and Mordred, their spells and poisoning from the Pleiades, that effectively thwarted Arthur and the Light.

The Avalon Priestesses, repeating the Saxon lifetime, were persuaded that the Goddesses could not stay on Earth, that they must be sent away for their own safety. The Saxon ritual was activated, as was the Orion dragon clone. Everyone died violently in that incarnation, as they had in the previous one. The men fell in the last battle against Mordred, and the women were poisoned by Morgause. The Goddesses were forced off the Earth completely and from this time forward could not return here. There would be no rejoining of Goddesses with their incarnations, and no ascension.

This is where it stood at the beginning of our own lifetimes, and a bleaker picture is not to be found. At the time of our births, most people had no memory of the Goddesses, much less of a way to be joined with them or become them. No one had heard of ascension or knew what it was. There was very little of the Light remaining on Earth. This was also, however, the generation of the sixties, the Harmonic Convergence and the new millennium, the women's movement, Women's Spirituality, and the New Age—and the astrologically predicted time of the Goddesses' return. Under these movements and in a very few years, we have learned a great deal and evolved very quickly. We have been given the return of the

Goddess in many ways, but not the Goddesses themselves. Many women have began to reach for Her.

Our Great Mother Nada in Her mercy decided to speed the evolution of Earth, and we were brought into contact with the Lords of Karma for this purpose. The usual cycle of karma resolving by repeated incarnations was effective but terribly slow. We were granted a period of karmic grace for the purpose of speeding up our karmic clearing. This was done because Orion and the evil Greys were an increasing threat to the survival of the planet. Their mechanisms and mutations in planetary and solar system creation, and in individual creations, were wreaking havoc with the environment and with human life. We were on the verge of being entrapped in another repetition of Mu or Atlantis, or another nuclear holocaust from our planet of origin. We were granted divine intervention and divine dispensation by the Light in an attempt to save the situation.

We were granted the ability to clear our own karma and the planet's by simple processes of approaching the Lords of Karma. At first, it was a temporary experiment to see what we would do with it, and then it was made permanent. When enough people knew about the Lords of Karma and were working seriously with them, a critical mass was reached. Karma could be ended on Earth and the karma of all people could be released. Once enough people—a very small number was required—had released *all* of their Earth karma, we were permitted to go further. We were given the request to reconnect the full complement of our DNA, reconnecting us to the memories and karma first of the Galaxy and then beyond. We were introduced to Divine Director.

By this time, it became abundantly clear that we were all under interdimensional attack, particularly against those first women whom Goddesses had approached and asked to reconnect with. The process of Galactic karmic clearing was a nightmare of psychic attacks, of cutting off from our Goddesses, and of psychic abilities repeatedly damaged and shut down. Piece by piece, however, we learned about Orion and the evil Greys and what they had done to us and to the Earth. We learned about reprogramming Creational Computers, met Light Mother and Tion and the protecting archangels, and discovered that the Light Ships were still with us. We discovered the Evil Twins of the Goddesses, having long been under fire from Evil Hybrids and their Evil Clans on Earth. It became very obvious that we were in a war, an interdimensional war involving frightening aliens and interstellar technologies.

We of Earth were definitely out of our league. But our Goddesses were being attacked and hurt along with us, and no one who knew about it could sit back and watch. If there is one thing that Goddesses do, it is to create a tremendous bond of love with their women. Few Goddess women would hesitate to risk their lives to protect a Goddess, especially their own. So we entered the war. First we screamed out for Archangel Michael and Divine Director every time something nasty came into our psychic perceptions. Then we started fighting back.

The day the word "annihilate" came into my mind with regard to something I was fighting, it frightened me. I didn't want to kill anything. According to Archangel Michael, however, it was just what I was supposed to do. He assured me I was not killing life, but the evil that threatens all life. I picked up the sword, and taught others to do the same, and together we fought the dark.

Eventually it became clear that we would not stop the attacks until we found and stopped their sources. One day on a New Moon, we made the request to Divine Director to destroy Orion, *all of it*. We could hear the Karmic Board applaud. We were shown it happening, when three beams or weapon rays of white light pierced the dark Orion ball. The ball boiled up like a black and smoking oil fire and dissolved as we watched. In the center was a roaring dragon, and we were told it was also to be destroyed. We received information on the dragon mutations, and that each planet has a life force dragon of the Light.

Next, we were shown the Orion dragon clone in the Earth, under the Atlantic Ocean. It was so large that it extended almost from one end of the planet to the other. We were told that the Goddesses were going to destroy it themselves, and we feared for their safety. We made requests to reduce the dragon, make it moribund, starve it of energy, and make the

Goddesses strong and invulnerable to harm. On the Full Moon, the Goddesses "killed" the dragon.

We were led step by step to make the requests of Divine Director to clear the Earth, Solar System, and Galaxy. We met the Shekinah and watched her cleanse the All, the Universe and Cosmos, of all the replications and regenerations of Lucifer. We found another Goddess to love, our Great Cosmic Mother of All. With the Shekinah, we learned about Na'ama and Lilith, and much later of Her other daughters. We learned about duality, and step by step we destroyed it: every Evil Twin, every Evil Hybrid, all the Mother Bodies, all the evil computers and evil grids, the Mastermind, all the members of the Conglomerate and Cartel (whose origin we weren't told about until almost the end). Eventually we came to the Ancient Evil and Evil God, to the Devil, Beelzebub, Satan, and Belial, and to the Evil Creator Spaceship. If we had known their real names at the time we destroyed them, we might have been too frightened to do so.

Bit by bit we learned who we are and where we came from, moving further and further out through the galaxies and Universe. We learned about Tion's valiant fight to protect the Light and save his planets from evil. We rescued the Shekinah's Consort and the Goddess Cybele. We learned about the Pleiades—some of us have gone there in dreams for almost a lifetime—and we learned about Orion and evil Grey interference with Earth's freedom. We remembered who we were on Orion and in King Arthur's court, and what was done to us in Atlantis and Mu. Step by step, each evil and member of the Chain of Evil fell to the justice of the Light. We watched it happen.

We discovered the satanic rituals that had been done to us, and the continuing effects of spells and curses made on other planets. We made the requests to destroy first the perpetrators and then the evil temples. The temples led us to our planet of origin, and we were at the end. Now we dealt with DNA mutations, Soul Matrix damage and shattering, the poison of nuclear fusion, and original mutations of the life force. We requested the resurrection of the Goddesses who had died, and of our souls in our own bodies. Again and again we requested rejoining with our Goddesses, requested protection and peace and safety, and the return of the Light.

Then we dealt with booby traps and fail-safes, attacks upon us by the automatic activations of evils whose perpetrators were long since gone. We found weaponry of destruction placed in our own hearts, programmed to detonate and destroy us and our Goddesses should our Goddesses come in, even weaponry that would destroy the Earth through us. We found circuitry of evil connecting one woman to another, one Goddess to another, connecting the components of our souls to make a domino effect of hate and devastation within us. There were nights we worked all night long to make the requests, and there were nights when we went to bed not knowing if something to kill us would activate by dawn. There were satellites and circuitry, transformers and activators, magnetics and electronics.

There were constant energy attacks, constant need for repairs in our own Be-ings, constant discoveries of the damage done to us and our Goddesses on every level, and constant damage to our souls. The Light repaired us and we fought again, making request after request to Divine Director and the Shekinah for healing and to end all evil at the source, from every source. There were only three of us fighting, and for many months we had been very much alone. It wasn't something you could tell your friends about, and most of our friends didn't want to know. It was the worst of despair and pain as we reached the end. Our bodies were worn out, and we were activating in them the damage of our souls. We were sick, exhausted, and in despair, too weak to go on. And then we were done.

We have been repaired, rebuilt, recreated, reconnected, restored, renewed, and resurrected, not only on Earth but throughout our Cosmos. Our Goddesses can come home now; they are safe and we are safe. We can be who we were meant to be. Spring Equinox 2001 is the beginning of the Age of Aquarius, the age of the Goddess. The Light has prevailed at last.

The Chain of Light

Who are the Be-ings that comprise the Chain of Light? *Essential Energy Balancing* introduced you to the Lords of Karma, your Energy Selves, and your Goddess. These are only the beginning of a network of many Be-ings with a great variety of duties and jobs. With the completion of Earth ascension, another level of Light Be-ings enters your awareness, usually our Great Mother Nada and Archangels Michael and Ashtar. With *Essential Energy Balancing II,* additional Light Be-ings will become known to you, primarily Divine Director, others of the Galactic Karmic Board, and more protectors of the Light. You may meet other Goddesses, including our Great Goddess Brede and our Light Mother, Judith. When you reach *Essential Energy Balancing III,* you will follow the Chain of Light to its end in our Cosmos, to the Cosmic Karmic Board and our beautiful Shekinah.

The Lords of Karma, whom you have already met, are composed of many groups of Ascended Masters, a different group for each soul. A soul is composed of all the incarnations under one Goddess's care. This means twenty-five or so oversouls and all the incarnations and Be-ings within them. Our oversouls are also our Goddess Selves. There are a minimum of seven and a maximum of eleven members of a Lords of Karma group, and the same group will appear to the same person for every request. There is often a spokesperson for the group, which the individual can learn to know and have rapport with. The Lords of Karma are both men and women, of all ages, types, cultures, and races. If you see them visually, they will usually appear in a way you can relate to, or they may appear to you in a way they feel you most need. If you imagine them as stern and unforgiving, they may either appear that way or appear as the opposite to reassure you. Some women describe very silly antics in their Lords of Karma groups, while others find them all seriousness. However they appear, they are to be treated with the greatest respect and regard. You are to take your work with them quite seriously.

When I first met the Lords of Karma, they appeared to me in dark robes with their faces hidden, their arms crossed over their chests; their body language was not reassuring. I made my request, heard the one-word answer "granted," and was afraid to approach them again. The healer who told me about them also warned me off, saying that they were only a last resort, only to be petitioned once in a lifetime—if then. Several years later, when they came to me and told me to "ask" with regard to karmic issues coming up in a tarot reading, they appeared to me in that way again. The more I worked with them and the more I asked, the less frightening and the more loving they became. We are to go to them with our requests as frequently as possible; it is now our job to do so.

One night during a workshop weekend, I made a request and in response heard the sounds of a party that was well underway. I asked what was happening and was told, "It's the end of karma." I had to ask them to repeat that, as I wasn't sure I had heard it correctly. It seemed too good to be true. Upon asking why, the answer was "critical mass, enough people are asking for karmic release to end karma on Earth forever." The party was still going on. From that time, the Lords of Karma have appeared in far less frightening ways to everyone who contacts them. They are gentle and nonthreatening in most cases, welcoming rather than forbidding. By reaching the critical mass they sought, we have proved to them our seriousness, our willingness and readiness to heal our karma and the planet's. They can relax with us now, and we can relax with them—to a point.

Each member of the Lords of Karma has completed ascension, the process of clearing and being released from all of their karma. This means not only Earth and Solar System karma, but their karma from all galaxies, universes, and cosmos as well. They are people just as we are, but far advanced

DIAGRAM 5

The Chain of Light

THE PLEIADES
CREATOR LIGHT SHIP

The Shekinah's Light

The Light, Sound, all
Vibrations, all Frequencies,
Energies of Creation

THE SHEKINAH
THE GREAT COSMIC MOTHER FOR THE UNIVERSE AND COSMOS

Cosmic Karmic Board
  St. Germaine (Head, Liaison for our Cosmos to the Creator Ship)
  El Morya (Liaison for our Galaxy to the Shekinah)
  Elohim (Archangels for the Cosmos), Astrea and Purity
Universal Protectors, Tion, Sanat Kumara, and Melchizadek
Universal Archangels, Metratron, Elijah

The Is and Is-Not
The Pure Light Beyond Creation

LIGHT MOTHER
THE ALL-MOTHER FOR OUR GALAXY (JUDITH)

Divine Director
(Liaison for our Solar System to the Galaxy,
Keeper of Galactic Karma)

Galactic Creational Computers
There is a Light Mother
for every galaxy

Galactic Archangels, Ashtar

The Radiance of the Light
Beyond the Goddess

NADA
THE GREAT MOTHER FOR THIS SOLAR SYSTEM (AND EARTH)

The Karmic Board
Guardians of the Four Directions:
  Archangels Michael, Gabriel, Raphael, Uriel

Nada is Keeper of the Void
and Non-Void and
of Earth Karma

BREDE
THE GREAT GODDESS (FOR EARTH)

The Lords of Karma
Guardian Angels
All Angels

Earth
All the
Goddesses

Brede is Keeper of the Earth
Grid and Creator of all Earth
Goddesses (Bridgit)

13 other Grid Keepers

CORE OF THE EARTH

Life Force of the Planet

(Pendragon, The Old One)

Earth Mother
Earth Dragon

of us in spiritual evolution. They have suffered and they've paid their dues, and they've prevailed against great adversity to clear and heal themselves. From the information in the past chapter, you begin to be aware of what the Light has seen and been through. You also are gaining awareness of how difficult ascension is to achieve. To be a member of the Lords of Karma, an Ascended Be-ing must have the desire to do this type of work. She or he is given advanced training for it, and to be chosen for the job is an honor. Our Great Mother Nada, who is the keeper of Earth karma and is its final authority, chooses who will be part of each Lords of Karma group.

The Lords of Karma are different from spirit guides. Spirit guides are Be-ings of higher development than those they serve, but they are usually not ascended. It is a job between lifetimes for those in service to the Light, who may be on the ascension path but have not yet completed it. Members of one's soul group, spirit guides are as much in training as the people they guide. They are not infallible. In other lifetimes, they may have been a loved one or a mate, but they only need to be a little more evolved than the person in body they work with. The primary job of a spirit guide is, as the name implies, to guide and advise one person, the person they are assigned to. Their job is to teach and to help the person evolve, to guide that person toward choices that are of the Light, and to keep her on the path of spiritual growth. The person they guide has free will, however. If you and your spirit guide disagree, you will make the choice and live with the consequences.

The Lords of Karma have an entirely different role. They are more like attorneys who intercede with the Light as advocates to secure and promote the soul's growth. They serve much more the entire soul than the individual of one incarnation. They seldom take the role of adviser, even when asked to; you do not ask them to guide you but to free you. The Lords of Karma are Be-ings with the authority to grant that freedom and release, if they feel you are ready to have it. They have access to all the Akashic Records of your soul, all the records of all your incarnations, and of all the karma you have accrued. They know where you have incarnated, how you have been damaged, and are aware of all the implications and complexities of every deed and incident in every one of your lifetimes. They are more evolved than spirit guides and they know you better, and the Lords of Karma also supervise your spirit guidance.

Decisions of what karma can be released and when are left to your Karmic Group. When you make a request, they have the authority to grant or refuse it based upon how much you have completed your understanding and healing of the issue, and met your responsibilities with regard to it. If you have learned what you need to of a situation, it is more readily released than a situation you are still repeating by your lack of comprehension. If you blame your circumstance on someone else, you are not likely to be granted release from it; if you understand your part in it and ask for help, you are likely to be released. The most important factor in receiving karmic release is in your realization that something is wrong in your life, that it needs healing, and that you need help to heal it. When you are aware of a pattern and ask to clear it, you are demonstrating your readiness for release.

Those who work the most frequently and thoroughly with the Lords of Karma earn their greatest respect. When you have the desire to heal yourself, to heal your life and lifetimes, and the willingness to face honestly what you need to know, you will have the help of the Lords of Karma to the utmost. Those who are willing to do the work of releasing their karma can release *all* of it; it is readily possible to do. The more seriously you work to do this, the more help you will have in doing so. If you desire the ascension path, you will be put upon it, and while the Lords of Karma do not advise per se, they will guide you on that path. They will make sure that you have the information you need to attain ascension. You will know what to ask for, and each request will lead you to the next and the next, until you have been shown all you need to know. As each piece of karma is released one piece at a time, you will be led ever deeper toward your goal.

Occasionally I have made a request to the Lords of Karma and received no response. They seem to leave, or if I'm using a pendulum, the action of the pendulum goes still. In these cases, your Karmic Group may be having a discussion about whether to grant your request or not. The response will come, usually in a few minutes, but sometimes it can take longer, even overnight. There are complexities to every request, and many ramifications. Sometimes the problem is that other things need to be freed first. If you are working with Divine Director on Galactic Karma, he may wish more precise words. On some of these occasions, the Lords of Karma may decide that they need a decision from higher up. For Earth karma, they may request judgment from Nada, who is the Great Mother creator of our Solar System and planet. Nada is the final authority for releasing Earth karma, and She aids us and intervenes for us with regard to karma from beyond this Solar System. Since we are Be-ings living in Her jurisdiction, She takes an interest in what we do. The further we proceed in clearing our Earth and Solar System karma, the more Nada becomes aware of us.

You will probably not meet Lady Nada until you have completed the processes of the first *Essential Energy Balancing* book and your clearing of Earth karma. Though you will have not yet seen Her, She will nevertheless have been aware of you for some time. If you are on the ascension path and seriously working toward it, you are under Nada's care. Nada appears psychically to me as a tall, almost gauntly thin, middle-aged woman with straight, long black hair and olive skin. She is always pregnant, though she seems past the age when most women bear children. In one of my first conversations with Her, I asked Her about it, and Her reply was, "All life is born through Me." She personifies the Goddess image that shows the Earth as the Goddess's pregnant belly. As keeper of planetary karma, Nada is also keeper of the Mind Grid of the Earth and Solar System, which are Creational Computers and our Akashic Records.

Nada has the authority to overrule your Lords of Karma group and either deny or grant you a disputed request. She can grant Karmic Grace to release you from something you may not have completed, to make it finished even if it isn't. Two of Nada's greatest attributes are Her practicality and Her mercy; She will find the simplest and gentlest way to accomplish anything at hand. When the wordiness of Divine Director becomes impossible for me, I ask for Nada, tell Her what I need, and it usually is done. She cuts the red tape for Earth karma and all karma beyond. She also takes the role of Mother for all the Goddesses who are coming to Earth. If your path of service includes the healing of the planet, you will work primarily with Nada, once your own Earth karma is finished.

The purpose of this book is the healing and release of Galactic Karma, and this means working with the Karmic Board and Divine Director. Everything I have said so far of the Lords of Karma also applies to working with the higher authority of the Karmic Board. They are even more eminent Ascended Be-ings who have been with us since our planet of origin. The Karmic Board is composed of Goddesses, the uncorrupted Twin Flames of Goddesses, and members of the Angelic Realm who are protectors of the Light. Nada, for example, is part of the Karmic Board, as are all the Goddesses coming to Earth, our Great Goddess Brede, and our Light Mother Judith. The Guardian Archangels of the Four Directions—Michael, Gabriel, Raphael, and Uriel—are members of the Galactic Karmic Board, as well as Archangels Ariel, Serafina, Ashtar, and others. There are about forty members of the Karmic Board at this level, besides the many Goddesses, compared with almost countless numbers of the Lords of Karma.

The member of this body whom you will work with for all processes and requests is Divine Director. He is the liaison between Earth and the Galaxy and between Earth individuals and Light Mother for the clearing of Galactic Karma. Divine Director is a title, not a name, but he is only one person. He was created by the Shekinah in our original cosmos and is the uncorrupted Twin Flame of a Goddess who was destroyed but is now being resurrected. He is a protector of the Light and has the status of a God, and of course is an Ascended Master. Divine Director has been a part of all the happenings of our creation and of our karma on every planet, including our karma on Earth and the karma of the planet itself.

Part of his job is to protect Light Mother and to protect and administer the workings of the Galactic Creational Computers, our individual and collective Akashic Records for the Galaxy. Included in Galactic Karma are all of our incarnations on a variety of Milky Way planets, including Orion, the Greys' planets, and Earth. Where our karma on Earth is affected by lifetimes from other planets, Divine Director's jurisdiction begins. These planets will partly include the Pleiades, which is classed as karma of the Cosmos, but do not include our planet of origin. Both are subjects of *Essential Energy Balancing III* and will be supervised by Divine Director, the Cosmic Karmic Board, Nada, and the Shekinah.

Galactic Karma is primarily managed by Divine Director with occasional input from Nada. Our Light Mother Judith is very pure and very innocent; She is kept highly protected and is only rarely involved. Judith is the creator Goddess of our Galaxy, and there is a Light Mother for each of the multitude of galaxies. Only Divine Director's permission is needed to edit the Galactic Creational Computers for an individual's karmic healing. If the healing is for our entire Galaxy, however, our Light Mother's permission is needed, along with the agreement of all of the Light Mothers from every galaxy in our Universe. It is Divine Director who will seek that permission, if needed, and Divine Director who is to be addressed. All the work of clearing our herstory, as described in the last chapter, was done with and through Divine Director.

The processes of this book are different in many ways from those of *Essential Energy Balancing* because of Divine Director's requirements. The Creational Grids or Computers (or Akashic Records) are the planetary and Galactic Mind Grids, and they are run by mental processes, which means they require the proper words to program them. Requests to Divine Director are highly formatted and sometimes very wordy. No aspect of a request can be skipped or taken as a given; what you state is what you get, so you must specify everything you need in exact detail. This can be onerous at times but it is necessary, and Divine Director will hold you to every last word and format. Every word is necessary since your words are reprogramming so vast a computer, the computer of your Galactic Karma. Your requests to him are legal contracts, the words of them are binding, and they must be accurate in every detail and nuance. If the Lords of Karma are attorney advocates, Divine Director is the judge of the Galactic court.

If you use a pendulum to work with the Lords of Karma, you may see something unusual when you do this with Divine Director. When he wants "more words"—when something is missing for a request to be complete—the pendulum will swing in a wide circle, neither yes or no. This is your clue that you are on the right track but haven't quite got it yet or do not have enough understanding for your request to be granted. Be aware of ideas coming into your head, and follow the leads of those ideas. This is how the information will be transmitted. Until you have all the words, all the understanding that is required for the full reprogramming, your request will not be granted or will be only partially granted. These demands are very different from those of working with the Lords of Karma, but Divine Director promises to make working with him as easy as possible. If you have understanding of legal terminology and processes, however, it will help!

Once you have cleared your Galactic Karma, there is also karma of the Universe and Cosmos (*Essential Energy Balancing III*). The next level of the Karmic Board operates here, the Cosmic Karmic Board. This is composed of all the members of the Galactic Karmic Board plus about another forty Be-ings, who again are Twin Flames, Goddesses, Ascended Masters, and Elohim. Elohim are advanced members of the Angelic Realm, created by the Shekinah for service to Her and to the Universe and Cosmos. The Cosmic Karmic Board includes those who left our original cosmos on the Creator Light Ship.

Among these are El Morya, who is the liaison to the Shekinah for our Galaxy, and St. Germaine, who is the liaison to the Creator Light Ship and its Be-ings for our Cosmos. St. Germaine is also the head of the Cosmic Karmic Board, with the title of Maha Chohan. He is the keeper of the Violet Ray of cleansing and purification that we are asked to call upon as often as possible. El Morya is the adviser for many of the Goddess unions. Other members of the Cosmic Karmic Board include Jesus, Kuthumi, Sanat Kumara, Lady Portia, Nada, Athena, Isis, Demeter, Kwan Yin, Brede, Melchizadek, Mary Magdalene, Tion, and the Shekinah's Consort. The Shekinah is the final authority in all requests that involve Universal and Cosmic Karma.

Beyond the Karmic Boards and even beyond the Shekinah is the Creator Light Ship. This is the space-going Mother Ship that brought us from our planet of origin to the Pleiades, and from the Pleiades to Orion, the Greys' planets, and finally to Earth. The high technology of our original creators is installed and preserved on the Creator Light Ship, and its primary purpose is for protection of the Shekinah and the Light. Some members of the Cosmic Karmic Board reside there, including St. Germaine, Melchizadek, Sanat Kumara, and members of the Elohim. Advanced weaponry for the protection of the Light resides on this Ship, and it is also the means by which our current Cosmos has again been sealed against the incursion of evil. It is the coordinating command center for all the forces of the Light when they need to fight.

The Creator Light Ship is the repository of the energies of life that comprise the Shekinah Herself and that She uses in Her creation. These include all aspects of Light, sound, frequency, vibration, energies of all types (known and unknown), and all creational energies, including the creation and generation of DNA. The Shekinah's Twin Flame Consort is the protector of these energies in particular, and of the Creator Light Ship and the Shekinah as well.

Protectors of the Light on all levels are another aspect of the Chain of Light. These begin with our Guardian Angels, who were created for Earth service only, and like our spirit guides they are assigned specifically to individuals. They are created by Nada, our planet's Great Mother, and are stepped-down energies from those of the Archangels and Elohim above them. Like the Lords of Karma, a specific group of angels is assigned to each soul and its incarnations. They are protectors and advisers, but may intervene only when given permission to by the person they serve. They cannot violate free will, and you must ask their help to have it. Along with all other aspects of the Chain of Light, angels were mutated to generate Evil Twins. These have now been destroyed with the mutation that caused them. As with people, angels were created at a lowered vibration to reduce the activation of the Evil Twins.

Archangels were created to serve the Solar System and Galaxy, and they were created by Nada. The two who are most familiar are Archangel Michael, who protects ascension path Be-ings through the dimensions, and Archangel Ashtar, who protects them between the dimensions. These two Be-ings were the Dimensional and Interdimensional Archangels for all the Goddess unions initially, but they now have been joined by other archangels in the protection of the total unions. Archangel Michael was incarnated as Lancelot at the time of King Arthur (he was never faithless with Guinevere), and he has incarnated on Earth since. His Sword transmits the Blue Light Ray of powerful protection.

Ashtar is a Light Ship commander and warrior of the Light, who works as a protector through the deeps of space and hyperspace, and between dimensions. He is a master of technology and the war against evil, and also a protector of ascension Be-ings and those on the ascension path. Ashtar's realms are the interspaces of the Solar System and Galaxy, and his Sword also transmits the Blue Ray. The archangels' weaponry are more than actual swords, of course; they are of a highly advanced technology brought with the Creator Light Ship from our original cosmos. All archangels are protectors of the Light and of the Goddesses.

Archangels of the Universe include Metatron and Elijah, who are also Twin Flames of Goddesses and who answer directly to the Shekinah. At this level are other protectors of the Light, as well, notably Tion, Sanat Kumara, and Melchizadek. Sanat Kumara resides on the Creator Light Ship, and he is the Twin Flame of the Goddess Parvati (Mother Goddess of India). His Sword transmits the Ruby Light Ray, used for the intensive purification of Be-ings at the soul level. The Ruby Ray is also an advanced weapon of protection for the Creator Light Ship, the Shekinah, and the Universe and Cosmos.

Melchizadek resides on the Creator Light Ship as its current pilot and master technician. (St. Germaine is its master navigator and mathematician, while Divine Director is the master computer programmer of the Galactic and Universal Creational Computers.) Melchizadek also wields the Ruby Light Ray, using it to purify the depths of space rather than for the clearing of individuals. He is an uncorrupted Twin Flame, whose Goddess was destroyed in our cosmos of origin and is now being resurrected by the Shekinah. He has the energy of someone who has kept himself apart from others and who has been very alone, and he is the original Hermit of the tarot.

Tion is a protector of the Universe and Cosmos who has figured prominently in our herstory. He has been a valiant defender and protector of the Light since the beginning and is known as a freedom fighter on many planets and in the Universe and Cosmos as a whole. He has been a major defender of the Earth and is sometimes known on Earth as Hermes or Thoth. Twin Flame of Athena, Tion and Athena were created directly by the Shekinah in our original cosmos. They were among the few to escape as a pair without mutational soul damage. Tion is a highly advanced technical scientist, the commander of a fleet of Light Ships, a military strategist, designer of weapons to serve the Light, rescuer of several planets and many Goddesses, destroyer of many evils, and a competent healer as well. (It is interesting to note that all the warriors of the Light are also healers.) He is the chief of armed forces of the Light and flies in every battle. Athena and Tion are the Shekinah and Consort of the Greys' planetary system and are members of the Cosmic Karmic Board.

Tion's Light Ship forces are piloted primarily by women, as are Ashtar's Ships. Some of the familiar names are Athena, Miriam, Aleya, Lorelai, Portia, Kali Ma, Diana, Artemis, Selene, Sarasvati, Inanna, and Lilith. These are all Goddesses, of course—Lorelai is an Elohim—and many others fly with Tion. The concept of Amazons probably originated with these Goddesses. Athena, Lilith, and Aleya are squadron leaders. Ariel fights with Ashtar's forces and grew up on Ashtar's Galactic Light Ship. The Light Ships are vast, as large as cities, and some Be-ings who are born and live on them never leave them. They are centers of technology and healing as well as of battle.

At the level of the Cosmos, the foremost protectors of the Light are the Elohim. These are archangels of the highest level, created directly by the Shekinah. They are Her protectors and agents, and are among the most powerful of the defenders of the Light. Though they were created in pairs, only some of the Twin Flames remain, and those who were mutated have been destroyed. Astrea and Purity, both female, are a pair of Elohim especially interested in aiding the Earth. They have been assigned by the Shekinah to extend the protections of the Goddess unions on Earth through the Universe and Cosmos. It must be noted here that while the first Twin Flame pairs were male and female, those who exist and remain (and are being re-created) today include female-female and male-male pairs. There has never been any censure by the Shekinah or any of the Light against same sex love and union. The word "elohim" means "the one and the many," and it translates directly from the Hebrew to mean "God with breasts."

This brings us back to the Goddesses and the Chain of Light itself, beginning with our Galactic Cord systems that are our individual extensions to the Chain of Light. In *Essential Energy Balancing* you met, and were merged and fused with, your Higher Self, Essence Self, and Goddess Self/Oversoul. The changes resulting from that joining and fusion created a channel of Light to connect you to your Goddess, by which She could enter, merge, and fuse with your energy. That channel is called the Galactic Cord. You are at one end and your Goddess is at the other; from there your Goddess is connected, and connects you, to the rest of the Chain of Light. If you bring in your Goddess, Her merging and fusion in your energy makes you *part* of the Chain of Light, not only connected to it, because you are joined with Her.

Much more information on the templates and chakra systems of the Galactic Cord is given in the last sections of *Essential Energy Balancing*. What is important to add here is that there are four portals involved in bringing a Goddess into your energy. If you are not bringing in a Goddess, these portals remain closed, but they will be developed all the same if you complete the clearing of your Galactic Karma. The portals are created when the energy bodies, chakra systems, and templates merge in the completion of your Earth ascension process. The portals are unified (combined or merged) templates.

The first of these portals is the Earth Portal, which contains two templates. This portal connects the Grounding Cord section of the Galactic Cord into and through the Planetary Grids, through the Well of Life and Fire of Life at the center of the Earth, and beyond them into the planetary core. If you are bringing in a Goddess, She connects with you through this portal and Grounding Cord even further, to tie into the Earth's life force dragon. At the physical body end of the Grounding Cord is the Earth Portal itself, the combined templates through which your Goddess union is opened.

The second portal is the Galactic Connection Point, or Moment of Self, located at the back of the heart system and going all the way through the heart from back to front. Your connection with your Goddess is a heart connection in every way. When this portal is open, it gives you sensory perception of your Goddess and gives Her full sensory perception through you of the Earth experience. A template within this portal, called the Heart Panels, opens these sensory perceptions. The receptacle that the Galactic Cord plugs into in your body is your Moment of Self. This is your creation point, the moment of Be-ing when your incarnation separated from your Goddess's Be-ing. The connection and opening of the Galactic Connection Point rejoins you with your Goddess and makes you whole.

Next is the Entrance Point, composed of two templates in the crown and throat chakras. This is where you and your Goddess are connected to the rest of the Chain of Light. When the Entrance Point is open, your Goddess is able to join Her energy with yours. It brings you into full contact with Her, and with the other members of the Light, the chain of creation that runs all the way to the Shekinah and even beyond. The opening of this portal, all four portals, is also necessary for sensory perception with your Goddess; if any of the four portals is closed (or hasn't been developed to open), you will not be able to see, hear, or touch your Goddess. She will be able to see and hear you, however.

The last of the four portals is the Ascension Portal, which consists of two Ascension body templates, the Celestial Template, and the Transpersonal Point, combined or unified. (See *Essential Energy Balancing* for more on all of these components.) The Ascension Portal connects you to your total union—the protectors and advisers of each Goddess union—and to your ascension itself. If you complete ascension without bringing in a Goddess, you will still have an Ascension Portal that is in full operation. When this portal is developed and open, it connects you to the rest of the Chain of Light. There are additional portals beyond the Ascension Portal that are part of ascension itself.

DIAGRAM 6

The Tube of Light/Galactic Cord (Soul Matrix)

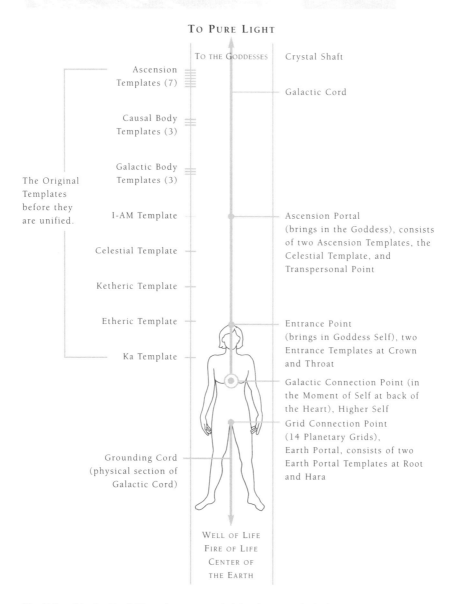

TO PURE LIGHT

TO THE GODDESSES — Crystal Shaft

Ascension Templates (7)

Galactic Cord

Causal Body Templates (3)

Galactic Body Templates (3)

The Original Templates before they are unified.

I-AM Template — Ascension Portal (brings in the Goddess), consists of two Ascension Templates, the Celestial Template, and Transpersonal Point

Celestial Template

Ketheric Template

Etheric Template — Entrance Point (brings in Goddess Self), two Entrance Templates at Crown and Throat

Ka Template

Galactic Connection Point (in the Moment of Self at back of the Heart), Higher Self

Grid Connection Point (14 Planetary Grids), Earth Portal, consists of two Earth Portal Templates at Root and Hara

Grounding Cord (physical section of Galactic Cord)

WELL OF LIFE
FIRE OF LIFE
CENTER OF
THE EARTH

The Tube of Light (Soul Matrix) is surrounded by the Crystal Shaft as its outer sheath and divided by the templates and energy bodies. The Galactic Cord runs through the center, from beyond the Pure Light to below the Center of the Earth. Four transformers bring the Galactic Cord into the physical: Ascension Portal (brings in the Goddess); Entrance Point (brings in Goddess Self); Galactic Connection Point (brings in Higher Self, and manifests Goddess and Goddess Self); and Grid Connection Point (all planetary connections and grids).

This is your Galactic Cord system, which connects you to the Chain of Light. The Chain of Light itself is the creation hierarchy of the Goddesses, extending from the core of the Earth through you and your Goddess, and through the Goddess lineage of the Earth, Solar System, Galaxy, Universe, and Cosmos—and beyond. The hierarchy of creation is slightly different for this Cosmos than it was for our cosmos of origin. Starting from the Earth, we begin with the life force, the planet's creational dragon of the Light, who is called Gaia. She was created at the inception of the planet by Nada, our Great Mother. Gaia in turn created Demeter, our Earth Mother, who is creator of the planet itself, its crystal and mineral composition, and all the life forms that live here.

Next in the Chain of Light are all Be-ings and all life, including our own lives, and all the Galactic Cord systems that connect us further to the hierarchy of Light. This means all that connects us to our Goddesses and all the Goddesses of Earth themselves. The Goddesses who were made for Earth were created by Brede, Earth's Great Goddess, and most of them were created in the Pleiades. They were created in conjunction with the women who had to be made in reduced form, who were soul aspects of the Goddesses and were to be rejoined with them. Most of the Goddesses created by Brede are Triple Goddesses. Some are Maiden, Mother, and Crone of the same Goddess, while some are three separate Goddess forms. A woman who brings in an Earth Goddess will have three Goddesses to live with! Please note that only Goddesses created *by Brede for Earth* are triple in form—Nada is not, for example, nor is Demeter or Brede Herself.

Brede was created by Nada and is a re-creation of both Lilith and Persephone. As Great Goddess, Brede is in charge of the Earth Grid, the energy system that maintains life on the planet. The Earth Grid is the power system that distributes the life force through all Be-ings on the planet and through the planet itself. Brede creates plants, animals, and people, and the spirits of their incarnations, but She does not create the souls themselves. The Shekinah differentiates souls. Brede creates the individuals rather than the life forms—your own dog, rather than the genus dog. She brings into form the manifestations of souls on Earth, and these are all in Her care and keeping. Some of Her favorite Be-ings are roses and pigs!

Nada is our Great Mother, the creator of our planet and Solar System. Among Her creations are our Solar System's Sun, our Moon, Earth's life force dragon of the Light Gaia, and Earth's Great Goddess Brede. Were other planets in our Solar System to be made to support life, Nada would create a dragon and a Great Goddess for each. Nada is the keeper of all karma on Earth and for this Solar System, and it is Her retrieval of the substance of life that Brede and Demeter work with. She maintains the Mind Grids of the planets and Solar System, which contain the Creational Computers and Akashic Records. She also creates the Mind Grids of each individual, her individual creations. Nada takes the substance of the life force from the Void and channels it through the Mind Grid, individual and collective, to turn the energy of thought into Be-ing. This creational thought energy is then put into form by other Goddesses. Please note also that all the Goddesses are creators of life and lives, no matter which Goddess in the Chain of Light created them. They take Nada's substance of life and put it into form.

With these Mind Grid duties, Nada is also the keeper of the Void and Non-Void. The Void is what Nada reaches into to retrieve the substance of life; it is organized chaos, all possibility, the positive dark. Nada's name is the Spanish word for "nothing"—She creates all life and Be-ing from "nothing." The planetary dragon, Earth Mother, and our Great Goddess take the thought substance of life from Nada's "nothingness" of the Void and give the substance form. This form is the Non-Void created from the Void. The Void and Non-Void are primary agents of creation, with Nada, Brede, Demeter, and Gaia the catalysts who turn one into the other. These are the jobs and duties of a Great Mother, Great Goddess, Earth Mother, and life force dragon: to take the substance of life (from the Void) and create life from it (manifestation, form, the Non-Void) by way of thought and the Mind Grid. It is how all things are born through Nada and why she is perpetually pregnant.

Between the Goddesses and Brede, between Brede and Nada, and between Nada and Light Mother (who is next on the Chain of Light) is the Radiance of the Light Beyond the Goddess, or simply the Radiance of the Light. All the Chain of Light is created, supported, and maintained by the Light, which is generated by the Shekinah from the raw materials brought to Her by the Creator Light Ship. This is the substance of the Goddesses' existence, even the Shekinah's existence, and the existence of all Be-ing. If the Light is shut off or destroyed, all Be-ing stops and would eventually disintegrate. We are Light made manifest, as are our Goddesses and all the Chain of Light.

Beyond Nada and the Radiance of the Light is the Galaxy and our Light Mother, or All-Mother, Judith. Light Mother creates in an ongoing way the Galaxy that supports and maintains all the solar systems and planets within it. There are many galaxies, each with a Light Mother. Each galaxy contains its own Creational Computers, Mind Grids, and Akashic Records, both individual and collective, in addition to those on the Earth and Solar System levels. There are additional Creational Computers for the Universe and Cosmos as well. Galactic Karma, again both individual and collective, is maintained in these structures.

The Galactic Creational Computers are also the repositories of the blueprints and programmings for all life forms that exist in each galaxy and in all the solar systems and planets of each galaxy. All the galaxies in a universe are connected by the network interface of these great Creational Computers. While individual Galactic Karma can be reprogrammed in these computers with the agreement of Divine Director, for collective Galactic Karma to be changed in any Computer requires the agreement of *all* the Light Mothers, not only the Light Mother of the galaxy involved.

A Light Mother incarnates only rarely, if at all. Our Great Mother Nada has incarnated on Earth frequently, as has our Earth Mother Demeter. Brede, as Great Goddess, has had several Earth incarnations, but far fewer than Nada or Demeter's lifetimes. A Light Mother may incarnate only once on each inhabited planet in Her galaxy. Judith's incarnation for Earth was Mother Mary. All of the Light Mothers are very young Maidens, children actually, and their innocence is fostered, protected, and cherished. The Radiance of the Light between Light Mother and the Shekinah is called the Pure Light Beyond Creation. The Light Mothers' purity depends on the purity of this Light, and it is strongly defended. The manifestation of creation from and through the Galaxy and Universe is called the Is and Is-Not. These are similar to Nada's Void and Non-Void but on a higher and more rarified level.

Beyond the Light Mothers is the Shekinah Herself, creator of souls, the Great Cosmic Mother of All in the Universe and Cosmos. She is our first Mother and our ultimate Mother. The Shekinah takes the raw materials of creation, collected for Her and channeled to Her by those on the Creator Light Ship, and turns them into the fabric of life and into the life of souls. These materials include all aspects of Light, sound, frequency, vibration, energies of a range of types, and a variety of creational processes known and unknown. Understanding of these raw materials and processes can only come from advanced physics, if at all in our present development on Earth. She is said to have created Herself from these energies as well.

The Shekinah weaves Light and turns that weaving into the warp and weft of life itself. Her Light is all the colors of the rainbow separately and together. Nothing of evil can withstand the intensity of the Shekinah's Light; evil is destroyed and melted by it like ice in the sun. Though stronger than the most powerful weaponry ever known, everything of Light is created by the Shekinah's Rainbow Ray. Both Her love and Her wrath are legendary primal forces. Traditional Judaism says that the Shekinah has come to Earth on only ten occasions and five of these were to punish the wrongdoings of Her people. Judaism also says that if a married couple is happy, the Shekinah rests between them to bless their peace. She is a force for good and the source of all good, but she can be a destroyer Goddess too, when destruction is necessary.

Traditional Judaism prays daily for the Shekinah to be reunited with Her Consort, stating that She fled Him when the Temple of Jerusalem was destroyed. The true story seems to be that when the Evil Twins first attacked the Light, they took the Shekinah's Consort captive. He was held that way for many centuries, and though He did not become an Evil Twin as so many of the Twin Flames did, a mirror image clone was made of Him who was evil.

This was Beelzebub, the Evil God. Much of the misogyny of Judaism was caused by this Evil God who came to Moses and others in the guise of Light.

The Shekinah was the first source, and She created Her Consort; it was not the other way around. The lies of the Evil God were the start of Patriarchy, as were the Evil Twins' attacks and destruction of the Shekinah's daughters, our first creator Goddesses. With the work that has been done to understand our herstory and clear the Cosmos and the All of evil duality, the Shekinah's Consort has been returned to Her. He has been cleansed and healed of all that was done to Him, and their union has been restored. Like others of the Goddesses' Twin Flames, He is a warrior and protector of the Light, and the Rainbow Light Ray He shares with the Shekinah is used as a weapon to consume all that is evil.

People on Earth are not to approach the Shekinah or speak to Her directly until they have achieved ascension, unless She approaches them first. To speak with Her, you must make your request through Divine Director or El Morya. El Morya was Moses in one of his Earth incarnations. When handled in this way, the Shekinah will hear and respond to your requests, though the response may not come from Her directly. Most requests do not need the Shekinah to resolve them; speak first with your own Goddess, Divine Director, or Nada. Nevertheless, our Great Cosmic Mother is a very lonely Goddess who has witnessed and suffered the greatest of tragedies. She wishes to be known and loved again as She once was, and feels She has been forgotten by the people She created. She still has interest and contact with the Hebrew people and Israel, and is aware of the political situation there. She is not pleased by what She sees.

The Shekinah is the Mother of souls and of Goddesses and is much involved with healing them and with clearing this Cosmos of the tragedies that came here with Her. She has needed healing Herself and is not yet fully recovered. She asks for and needs your love, She who is love Herself, as do all the Goddesses and all the Chain of Light.

Before You Begin

From now on you will ask for Divine Director and the Lords of Karma, or Divine Director and the Karmic Board, for all requests. The Be-ings who appear when you do so will be different from those you have met before. The processes of this book are different from those in *Essential Energy Balancing,* as they are all Lords of Karma requests instead of meditations. Like the *Essential Energy Balancing* processes, however, those of this book are reprogrammings of your karma, this time of your individual karmic computers (Akashic Records) on the Galactic level. This is Galactic Karma instead of the Earth karma you are familiar with. The requests directly reprogram the Galactic Creational Computers, and they must be done in the order and exact format in which they are given.

These requests are more complicated than those in *Essential Energy Balancing.* You are not expected to memorize the formats but can do them from the book as you read. Add your own requests by using the same formats, substituting your request for the request stated in the process. There is no need to be in a lying down position or to do these reprogrammings in full meditation mode. There is no particular time or place that is best for most of these, but your focus should be uninterrupted. As long as you do them sequentially, you may do as many processes at one sitting as you wish. You may also do as many additional requests as you choose by using the formats in the book, and you may do as many at a time as you want to.

Though these processes are very word oriented—and you must keep the wording exact—you will feel them in your body and energy. They have a resonance that goes beyond the words them-selves. Once you do each one, as you do it and after, you will feel that resonance continue for some time. From the time you make each request, or group of requests, it can take as short as a few minutes or as long as two weeks for the reprogramming of the Galactic Creational Computers and the rest of your own energies to take place. There will be periods during this time when your crown chakra may be closed, causing you to feel shut down and unable to access your psychic abilities. Consider these times to be healings and just wait for them to clear. They will not hamper your daily life.

When you ask to "cancel all karma and all karmic contracts" in a request, the period of reprogramming and your closing up takes four hours. You may do a number of these requests at one time to get them all completed together, or do the requests at bedtime before sleep so that they are finished by morning. If you do a large number of requests at once, which I recommend, the period of closing can be longer than four hours, but you will also have accomplished more. I suggest making every request you can think of at a session, for the purpose of faster completion overall.

When you do Process XVIII: Re-Creation and Replacement, you may experience closing up for five days or longer. This process, however, is the most important in the series, and the healing it offers is worth the wait. While your Crown is closed, you may continue to make requests, but for the Re-Creation and Replacement only it is best to wait until you are reopened before going on. This closing up, needless to say, is a profound healing of your life and your karma, and, though uncomfortable, it will do you no harm.

You will discover that when you make a request to Divine Director, a second related request will pop into your head immediately. When you make the second request, a third request will occur to you. These leads are extremely important to follow. Make every request that comes into your mind. It is best to do this immediately when the thought comes. If you don't do it, the thought will fade and be lost within seconds, and these thoughts are extremely important. If you are unable to

do the request when the thought occurs, make a no*
Don't expect to remember the request, you won't *
keep a list of these requests all day and make the
evening if you wish to, or whenever you have the time.
them immediately, or write them down as soon as each occurs to y*
you will lose them.

Another thing unique to these processes is that once you begin the format and words for these requests, you may forget what you asked for. By the time you finish a process, you may not remember what the request was that you made. This is not a sign of debility on your part, it just seems to work that way. Again, you can write down the request before you make it, or just do it and don't worry about remembering. It is less important to remember than to do the work. These processes are Mind Grid reprogrammings. You are asking to remove from your Mind Grid (and then from your karma, Galactic Creational Computers, and Akashic Records) some aspect of the programming of your Mind. Karma is a programming of the Mind. Your request asks that you remove something, and it is removed even from your memory. This can be disconcerting, but it is how the reprogramming works and is not a symptom of something being wrong with you or with the process.

I should not need to say it, but it bears mentioning that you are to treat Divine Director and all other Karmic Board Be-ings with the utmost respect. They are offering you healing never before possible of things in your lifetimes on many planets that have been impossible to clear until now. The processes required are wordy and can be frustrating—my own patience with all the words has given out many times—but all those words are really needed. If you are familiar with computer language and programming or with the language of legal contracts, you will understand the similarities. The complexities are not Divine Director's fault but are how the reprogrammings must be done. If it were not necessary to make things so involved, I assure you it would all be written more simply.

With every request, remember to say "thank you." If you are denied a request, see if you have left something out of the process or try changing wording. A "no" response can also mean that something else must be released first. Once that something else is done, you will be granted your original request. If you can hear Divine Director, you can simply ask him what needs to be done. If you use a pendulum, your skill at asking the right questions will be honed to an art. Pay attention at all times to the things that just seem to pop into your mind. That's where the answers will be.

Occasionally you will receive a "no" response because a request is already done or not needed. At one point in my own work, I continued to receive a "no" to something I felt to be important. I eventually became frustrated and told Divine Director that I was going to keep asking until it was granted. I heard the Karmic Board clapping! Eventually I got the "yes" after a lot of other things were cleared. I also had much more understanding of the problem by that time, which was probably the point. The reason to do these processes, and make these requests to Divine Director, is to heal and release *everything*. Keep going until you do so, and it will heal your life.

I have no intention of scaring anyone off by these warnings of complexity. What was most complex was the development of these processes, which went through dozens of rewrites until Divine Director was satisfied with each. They are there in front of you in writing, and you have only to do them as you read them. Once you do each request, you can add as many of your own to it as you can think of. When you get into the Short Process (XI), you will have a reasonably simple format for all requests, and this may be the one process you wish to memorize. Most of these processes are to be done only once, you will not need to repeat them. Likewise, requests of your own, particularly if you do them in the Short Process format, only need to be done once for each.

One more thing that you need to know about Divine Director is that you may make requests of him for others. With his full knowledge of all karma in all individuals, he will decide whether your request for someone else can be granted. The Lords of Karma in your original Earth Karma Group will only grant requests for *you*. This is different in that you may ask Divine Director for healing or help for others and receive it without their participation—if it is for their best good, in accordance with their karma and path, and if Divine Director agrees. In this case, if the answer is "no," you must accept the "no." He is the final authority. You may find ways to help others through these requests, and it can feel very good to do so.

To begin these processes, first ask for the full reconnection of your DNA. You will not be able to work with Divine Director otherwise, or access the Galactic Creational Computers to do the reprogramming of your Galactic Karma. This is the most important request of *Essential Energy Balancing II,* and we will do it in a moment. It only needs to be requested once, though it will take some time to complete. You may make this request also for your pets and children, and it would be of great benefit to them as well. Your number of DNA strands before you began to clear your Earth karma was only two strands. With *Essential Energy Balancing,* you requested reconnection to twelve strands, and at the end of clearing your Earth karma to twenty-one strands. These additional DNA strands, by the way, will not show up in a microscope; they are other-dimensional.

With the request that follows, you will ask to reconnect *all* your DNA strands. The number of strands in the full complement of DNA will vary with the individual. Eighty-one strands is the highest number possible; it is the Goddesses' number that they and we were created to have by the Shekinah. The number that is complete for you will vary according to your life path, your soul evolution, and your ascension level. The numbers will continue to increase as you release more and more of your Galactic Karma, and increase still more if you continue to clear your karma from the Universe and Cosmos. Where your clearing stops, the reconnection stops. As that is the only limit, the rest is up to you.

You will contact Divine Director in the same way that you already contact the Lords of Karma. Simply ask for his presence in a focused state of mind, and look and listen within. You may use a pendulum to see if you have made the contact and to receive your "yes" and "no" responses. Take a moment now to do this, and ask to speak with Divine Director and the Lords of Karma. It is Divine Director who will be the spokesperson now. When you have made contact with him, make the following request.

1. Ask to clear, heal, reconnect, and fully activate the full complement of your DNA.

2. Thank Divine Director and the Lords of Karma.

You will receive a "yes" or "no" response. No further words or process are needed. This is the simplest request of *Essential Energy Balancing II* and the most important. The process will commence immediately and be ongoing.

No one will be refused this request, but you may be told that something else must be done or asked for first. Ask what it is, or if you already know or it comes into your mind, do what is needed. This usually means asking to clear something you are shown; make the request to Divine Director and the Lords of Karma. When it is granted, ask for the DNA reconnection again. It will usually be a "yes." This is the same way you learned to release a "no" response with the Lords of Karma, and it is how to release a "no" at any time with Divine Director too.

You may wish to ask for the DNA reconnection for your animals and children, as both are aspects of your own soul. They will go through the ascension as you do, just by being around you. I have discovered something important about pets with these processes. If a dog or cat that was very close to you has died and you wish to have that animal back again, there are procedures for doing this. When you get your next new animal, whether it is a small puppy or kitten or a full-grown dog or cat, you can make the requests that will enable your lost pet to reincarnate into the new animal. This means asking that the aspect of your soul that was in your dead pet now join with a new body. Your old pet must agree to this and want to come back to you at this time.

Our pets take on an aspect of our souls automatically; it is part of the service they do for us and their means of bonding with us. If you get a young puppy or kitten, yours is the first soul aspect they will have, and the only aspect if you keep the pet for life. If you get an older animal, yours may be its second or third soul aspect. If your grown pet has had other owners, the last owner's soul aspect will leave and yours will enter in about six weeks after bringing the animal home. A young puppy or kitten will take on the soul aspect more quickly. So far, all of this happens unrequested. When you adopt an older animal that becomes a behavior problem, the reason is that the pet refuses to let go of its first owner's soul aspect or refuses to let yours in. This usually happens from grief or insecurity, or with an animal that has been abused.

So far you haven't had to do anything. To bring a specific soul aspect into a new pet (and it must be a new pet, one you have had for less than a week), you can make the requests that follow to Divine Director and the Lords of Karma. You must also be able to pass Reiki attunements or have someone available to pass them for you. Your third requirement is to have on hand Process I of *Essential Energy Balancing,* the opening meditation on page 84 of that book.

With these things and your animal in the room, place your hands on your pet and ask to speak with Divine Director and the Lords of Karma. If you are using a pendulum for this, one hand on the dog or cat will do. When you make the contact:

1. Ask to clear, heal, reconnect, and fully activate the full complement of DNA for your pet.

2. Ask that your departed pet (name) be permitted to reincarnate in your new animal, if your first pet is willing. You will receive a "yes" or "no."

3. Ask for a name for your new animal and listen for the answer. It may or may not be the name of your old pet.

4. Give your new animal three Reiki attunements, Reiki I, II, and III. Do this over the pet's crown; there is no need to manipulate the paws as you would on a human. Just make sure that all the symbols are drawn.

5. Wait three days, then do *Essential Energy Balancing* Process I for your pet. Ask to speak with Divine Director and the Lords of

Karma, and read the process for your pet while touching her, leaving some space between the steps.

6. Follow any further instructions the Light may give you.

7. Thank Divine Director and the Lords of Karma. The Light will do the rest.

Please understand that your new pet, even as a reincarnation of your old friend, will not be a carbon copy of the animal that has died. In a puppy, you may not see the old dog in the new one until it is older. In an older dog or puppy, watch for characteristic traits that will tell you that your old animal is there. Your new pet may or may not want to carry the same name she had before. If you are able to communicate psychically with your animal, you can discuss the name with her. This regard for her wishes in the matter is especially reassuring and comforting to a grown dog or cat. I have done this twice now with my dogs, and I can tell you that it works, and that it is a very great gift.

Before you begin the Galactic Karma processes, make one more request to Divine Director and the Lords of Karma or Karmic Board. Like all requests, it is a programming of your mind. So many people in today's New Age have so many different ideas of what ascension is that a definition of what is expected is required. Some people think—so many that I felt it necessary to clarify this—that by completing ascension they are going to die or disappear into a new dimension, taking their bodies with them. What is in your mind is what you create and what you draw from the Void, in the same way that Nada draws all things from the Void by means of Her Mind. The process that follows is a definition for the benefit of telling your mind, Mind Grid, Creational Computers, and Akashic Records exactly what you want to happen.

If you have completed *Essential Energy Balancing,* you have completed your requirement for Earth incarnation. In *Essential Energy Balancing II,* you begin to complete, and will ultimately end, your requirement for incarnation on all planets. However, you are incarnated in a body at this time, and your body and your lifetime in that body must be protected. In

Essential Energy Balancing, you made the request that you not le.
body until your full incarnation is finished. In *Essential Energy E*
II, a similar and further request must be made before you proceed.

Ask to speak with the Lords of Karma, Divine Director, and the Karmic
Board, and make the following statement:

1. I ask that my ascension and all ascension processes be completed
   while in my body on Earth and that I remain alive and in my body
   after ascension for the period of my full incarnation.

2. I also ask that I not end my incarnation on Earth with my ascension, but that I remain incarnated until this lifetime is completed.

3. Wait for a response. No one will be refused, but you may be given
   further instructions. Follow them. A full Lords of Karma process
   is not needed with this request at this time.

4. Thank the Lords of Karma, Divine Director, and the Karmic
   Board. You are now ready to begin the processes of this book.

A revised version of the *Essential Energy Balancing* Daily Clearing
(Process II) follows. This is a more advanced version with Divine
Director that takes into account all the changes that have happened in
your energy as a result of your Earth ascension and the fusion of your
Higher Self, Essence Self, and Goddess Self. This process is to be done
as often as possible unless your Crown is closed. Otherwise, doing it
daily is not too often. You may wish to tape this meditation and use it at
night upon going to bed. The full clearing can take up to an hour and
you are welcome to sleep through it. Once you have done this new version several times, you may simply ask Divine Director and the Lords of
Karma to start an Essential Energy Balancing for you, and then go to
sleep. They will understand that you mean the advanced process. If you
are bringing in a Goddess, make the request (and all requests) for you,
your Goddess, your union, total union, and your ascension. Then begin
the process.

Revised Daily Practice Total Energy Clearing

Ask for the Lords of Karma and Divine Director with each step, and allow the clearing for each step to complete before going to the next. The step is finished when you feel the energy reach your feet. If, at any step, it feels as if the energy is stopped or not moving, ask what may be wrong. Is there blockage or obstruction here? Is something disconnected, damaged, needing healing, repair, or replacement? Ask for what is needed. Do you simply need to wait longer for the clearing to finish? Use this process as an all-energy diagnostic system as well as for all-energy clearing.

Since you have completed all the processes of *Essential Energy Balancing,* all of your Energy Selves are merged into your Goddess Self, and your Goddess Self is merged into you. There is no need to call them in at the end of the energy clearing; they are already there. There is also no longer need to clear your Silver Cord once your Energy Selves are fully merged. As your Galactic Cord is formed to take its place, the Silver Cord becomes part of it. The new steps of this process reflect your new energy components, developing since your Earth ascension was completed.

1. Ask the Lords of Karma and Divine Director to clear, heal, align, open, activate, synchronize, fill with Light, repair and reconnect your:

   ENTIRE TUBE OF LIGHT AND CRYSTAL SHAFT,
   and all chakras, chakra complexes, channels, connections, and templates on all levels, all chakra systems, and all systems.

2. Ask the Lords of Karma and Divine Director to clear, heal, align, open, activate, synchronize, fill with Light, repair and reconnect your:

   GROUNDING CORD ON ALL LEVELS TO THE CENTER OF THE EARTH AND BEYOND, INCLUDING THROUGH ALL PLANETARY STRUCTURES, GRID STRUCTURES, AND ALL CONNECTIONS, and all chakras, chakra complexes, channels, connections, and templates on all levels, all chakra systems, and all systems.

3. Ask the Lords of Karma and Divine Director to clear, heal, align, open, activate, synchronize, fill with Light, repair and reconnect all:
    TEMPLATES ON ALL LEVELS,
    and all chakras, chakra complexes, channels, and connections on all levels, through all systems.

    List the following templates one by one, going to the next only after the previous template is cleared. Keep them in strict order.

    a) Ka template
    b) Etheric template
    c) Ketheric template
    d) Celestial template
    e) I-AM template
    f) All Galactic chakras and templates on all levels
    g) All Causal Body chakras and templates on all levels
    h) All Ascension chakras and templates on all levels.

4. Ask the Lords of Karma and Divine Director to clear, heal, align, open, activate, synchronize, fill with light, repair and reconnect your:
    HEART COMPLEX, HEART PANELS, AND ALL HEART SYSTEMS ON ALL LEVELS,
    and all chakras, chakra complexes, channels, connections, and templates through all of these, all chakra systems, and all systems.

5. Ask the Lords of Karma and Divine Director to clear, heal, align, open, activate, synchronize, fill with Light, repair and reconnect your:
    PHYSICAL AND ETHERIC BODIES,
    and all chakras, chakra complexes, channels, connections, and templates on all levels, all chakra systems, and all systems.

List the following chakras one by one, going on only after the previous chakra is fully cleared.

a) CROWN CHAKRA, chakra complex, and chakra system on all levels, all systems

b) THIRD EYE CHAKRA, chakra complex, and chakra system on all levels, all systems

c) THROAT CHAKRA, chakra complex, and chakra system on all levels, all systems

d) HEART CHAKRA, chakra complex, and chakra system on all levels, all systems

e) SOLAR PLEXUS CHAKRA, chakra complex, and chakra system on all levels, all systems

f) BELLY CHAKRA, chakra complex, and chakra system on all levels, all systems

g) ROOT CHAKRA, chakra complex, and chakra system on all levels, through all systems, to the center of the Earth and beyond, including through all planetary structures and grid structures.

6. Ask the Lords of Karma and Divine Director to clear, heal, align, open, activate, synchronize, fill with Light, repair and reconnect your:

EMOTIONAL AND ASTRAL BODIES,

and all chakras, chakra complexes, channels, connections, and templates on all levels, all chakra systems, and all systems.

List the following chakras one by one, going on to the next only after the previous chakra is cleared. Keep them in order.

a) TRANSPERSONAL POINT CHAKRA, chakra complex, and chakra system on all levels, all systems

b) VISION CHAKRAS (2), chakra complex, and chakra system on all levels, all systems

c) CAUSAL BODY CHAKRA, chakra complex, and chakra system on all levels, all systems

d) THYMUS CHAKRA, chakra complex, and chakra system on all levels, all systems

e) DIAPHRAGM CHAKRA, chakra complex, and chakra system on all levels, all systems

f) HARA CHAKRA, chakra complex, and chakra system on all levels, all systems

g) PERINEUM CHAKRA, chakra complex, and chakra system on all levels, through all systems, to the center of the Earth and beyond, including through all planetary structures and grid structures

h) MOVEMENT CHAKRAS (2), chakra complex, and chakra system on all levels, all systems, to the center of the Earth and beyond, including all planetary structures and grid structures

i) GROUNDING CHAKRAS (2), chakra complex, and chakra system on all levels, all systems, to the center of the Earth and beyond, including through all planetary structures and grid structures

j) EARTH CHAKRAS (2), chakra complex, and chakra system on all levels, all systems, to the center of the Earth and beyond, including through all planetary structures and grid structures.

7. Ask the Lords of Karma and Divine Director to clear, heal, align, open, activate, synchronize, fill with Light, repair and reconnect your:

MENTAL BODY AND MIND GRID,

and all chakras, chakra complexes, channels, connections, and templates on all levels, all chakra systems, and all systems.

List the following chakras one by one, going to the next only after the previous chakra is cleared. These chakras are not Kundalini (etheric body) chakras, but their mental body and Mind Grid counterparts.

    a) CROWN CHAKRA, crown complex, crown system on all levels, all systems

    b) THIRD EYE CHAKRA, third eye complex, third eye system on all levels, all systems

    c) LIGHT CHAKRAS (2), Light complex, Light system on all levels, all vision systems, all systems

    d) Chakras at the TOP OF THE THROAT, LIPS AND LOWER THROAT, AND ENTIRE THROAT COMPLEX, the throat system on all levels, and through all systems

    e) SOLAR PLEXUS CHAKRA, solar plexus complex, solar plexus system on all levels, all systems. (Note: there is no heart or heart equivalent on the mental body or Mind Grid levels.)

    f) ROOT CHAKRA, root complex, all root systems, all systems, to the center of the Earth and beyond, through all planetary structures and grid structures

    g) All chakras, chakra complexes, chakra systems on all levels and through all systems of the BREASTS, FINGERS, AND TOES.

8. Ask the Lords of Karma and Divine Director to clear, heal, align, open, activate, synchronize, fill with Light, repair and reconnect your:

    SPIRITUAL, GALACTIC, AND CAUSAL BODIES,

    and all chakras, chakra complexes, channels, connections, and templates on all levels, all chakra systems, and all systems.

    The chakras for these are as follows, in sets rather than individually.

    a) All chakras, chakra complexes, chakra systems on all levels and through all systems for the chakras of WILL, DESIRE, ATTAINMENT, ACTION, AND PROPULSION, to the center of the Earth and beyond, through all planetary structures and grid structures. (These are the galactic body chakras.)

b) All chakras, chakra complexes, chakra systems on all levels, and all systems for the chakras of SOUND, RECEPTION/ INFORMATION, COMMUNICATION, MANIFESTATION, CREATION, and IMPLEMENTATION. (These are the causal body chakras.)

c) THE SPIRITUAL, GALACTIC, AND CAUSAL BODY CROWN CHAKRA, crown complex, crown system on all levels and through all systems.

9. Ask the Lords of Karma and Divine Director to clear, heal, align, open, activate, synchronize, fill with Light, repair and reconnect your:

ASCENSION ON ALL LEVELS,

and all the chakras, chakra complexes, channels, connections, templates, and components of all ascension processes through all systems.

(Note: The ascension processes operate through all the bodies. To request clearing for only the Ascension Body would be to limit this request for clearing.)

10. When the ascension levels are fully cleared, the energy clearing is complete. Thank the Lords of Karma and Divine Director. This process is best done lying down at night before sleep. Follow it with an Essential Healing Circle if you wish (*Essential Energy Balancing* after Process V, page 103), or a night's sleep.

One last comment before you begin (actually you have already begun) the twenty-four processes of *Essential Energy Balancing II*: there needs to be a brief discussion about negative interference and fear. The things you will be clearing yourself of in the processes that follow require that you recognize the existence of evil and what it has done to your life on Earth and on other planets. Many people refuse to recognize or acknowledge these things simply because it is just too scary to do so. Once you acknowledge their existence, you have to be aware of them, and that means opening fears you would rather let be. It means opening memories from past lives and this life that are decidedly unpleasant. Yet this is the focus of Galactic Karma, specifically the discovery and clearing of negative interference and evil.

When these incidents of evil happened in your life, in this or other lifetimes, on Earth or other planets, you had no way to protect yourself or stop them from happening. You were helpless then, but you are no longer helpless. The processes in this book are your way of clearing and healing yourself of all the wrongs that have happened to you in your Galactic and Earth lifetimes. If the idea of evil is distasteful, there is something there you need to know. The things you resist the most have the most to tell you. They also offer the highest opportunities for change and healing. And when you work with Divine Director, the healing that happens prevents what is cleared from ever happening to you again.

Therefore, no matter how scary some of these things may be, and no matter how much your self-preservation instincts tell you to run away, you will be doing yourself great good to stick with it. Denial of evil, hiding from what happened to you, is like a child hiding in a closet from a fire in her bedroom. She may hide, but she risks her life in doing so—the fire will not go away because she can't see it, and there is still a great deal there to hurt her. I ask you to bear with me in these processes and to clear your Galactic Karma of all that can hurt you, so it can never hurt you again.

With that said, let us begin the *Essential Energy Balancing II* processes and the release of your Galactic Karma.

The Processes

Process I   Earth Karmic Contracts

THIS PROCESS AND THE NEXT ONE ARE PARTLY A REVIEW. USE THEIR formats for all things not yet healed in your life by your work with the first *Essential Energy Balancing* book and the Lords of Karma. These processes can also be used to cancel karmic contracts with a person—use carefully. Do the following request, as well as those listed as Universal Healings at the end. You should have already completed all the Universal Healings of *Essential Energy Balancing* as well; if you haven't, go back and do them now. The wording of all of these processes is very precise, ask exactly as written.

Note: If you have completed *Essential Energy Balancing* and know that you are bringing a Goddess into your energy, include the following in all requests for all processes: for you, your Goddess, your union, total union, and ascension.

1. Ask to speak with Divine Director and the Lords of Karma.

2. Ask to CANCEL ALL KARMA AND ALL KARMIC CONTRACTS through all lifetimes with ALL VOWS, AGREEMENTS, AND PROMISES NO LONGER GOOD FOR YOU TO KEEP.

    If the answer is "no," ask what you need to do to have this healing. If you are given a reason, the reason often becomes another Lords of Karma and Divine Director process. Clear the reason with another request process, then ask again. If you are told that you don't need the requested healing, there is no reason to go further, but this will be for only a very few people.

3. If the answer is "yes," ask for the healing through your:
   Mind Grid level
   DNA level
   Karmic contract level
   Core soul level and beyond
   Ascension level

   If the answer is "no" for any of these, ask first if the healing is needed at this level—it may not be and if not, continue. If the answer is "no" and a release is needed, ask what to do to proceed. Clearing the "no" may require another Divine Director and Lords of Karma request; complete the clearing request, then come back to the current question.

4. When you have a "yes" to all of the above outer levels, ask for the healing:
   From beyond your Moment of Self to below the Center of the Earth and
   From below the Center of the Earth to beyond your Moment of Self

   If the answer is "no," ask what you need to do to clear the "no" before going on.

5. When the answer is "yes," ask to seal the healing unto the Light and unto protection forever. If the answer is "yes," go on. If the answer is "no," it is either not needed or not appropriate for your current request. Go to the next step either way.

6. Ask for the healing through:
   All the levels and all the bodies,
   All the lifetimes including the present lifetime,
   Heal all the damage,
   And bring the healing into the present NOW.

7. If the answer is "yes," the process is complete. If the answer is "no," go through the lines one by one asking for "yes" or "no" with each. Find the part of the request that is denied, and ask what you need to do to clear the "no." Do what is required—it may mean further Lords of Karma and Divine Director requests to release a lifetime or situation—then ask again for the item that was refused. When all parts of the process achieve a "yes" response, the process is finished.

8. Thank the Lords of Karma and Divine Director.

9. It takes approximately three weeks for a healing sealed unto the Light to be completed. You will feel gradual changes in your energy but usually few symptoms. Once granted, know that it is done.

10. You may do as many of these requests and processes at a time as you wish to do, and do them as often as you think of things to clear. There is no need to wait between requests.

Universal Healings Ask to cancel all karma and all karmic contracts with each of the following items:

    a) The Negative Form in all its manifestations
    b) All manifestations and sources of evil and their negative effects
    c) All fear from all sources and fear's negative effects
    d) All guilt from all sources and guilt's negative effects
    e) The loss of your full empowerment
    f) All obstacles and obstructions to your life path from all sources

Use this process for everything in your life that needs healing, one request at a time. The key term is to "cancel all karma and all karmic contracts" with each. Remember to thank Divine Director and the Lords of Karma with all requests.

Process II Earth Negativity

EARTH NEGATIVITY IN THE REQUESTS BELOW REFERS TO THE PLANETARY MASS consciousness and how it affects your thinking and your life. We live immersed in media sensationalism that puts all the worst of human nature and planetary destruction in our awareness at all times. All that is negative around us is forced upon us twenty-four hours a day. We have learned suspicion of other people and that all events are disasters, and we have learned to live in fear. Joy never makes the daily news. Such a weight of fear and negativity affects us, and it affects those around us. Some people react to it by lashing out at others—by sending out their fear in the form of greed, hatred, jealousy, and other negative emotions, directed specifically at individuals or just in general. This bombardment stays with us, and it pulls us down. The process that follows attempts to separate and protect you from that constant bombardment of planetary fear.

Once you have learned Short Process XI, use it to repeat the following requests. Doing so will extend the healings below to EARTH AND ALL PLANETS.

If you are bringing in a Goddess, make sure to make all requests for you, your Goddess, your union, total union, and your ascension.

1. Ask to speak with Divine Director and the Lords of Karma.

2. Ask to CANCEL ALL KARMA AND ALL KARMIC CONTRACTS WITH ALL EARTH NEGATIVITY, all Earth grid negativity, all negative planetary mass consciousness, all violence, and the negativity of all people (including others' jealousy, greed, envy, malice, hatred, harm, and negative interference toward you).

3. If the answer is "yes," ask for the healing through your:
    Mind Grid level
    DNA level
    Karmic contract level

Core soul level and beyond

Ascension level

4. When all responses are "yes," ask for the healing:

    From beyond your Moment of Self to below the Center of the
    Earth and

    From below the Center of the Earth to beyond your Moment
    of Self.

5. If the answer is "yes," ask to seal the healing unto the Light and
    unto protection forever.

6. Ask for the healing:

    Through all the levels and all the bodies,

    All the lifetimes including the present lifetime,

    Heal all the damage,

    And bring the healing into the present NOW.

7. When the answer is "yes," thank the Lords of Karma and Divine
    Director.

8. Repeat this process for the following requests:

    a) Ask to raise your physical and etheric body vibrational lev-
        els above all Earth negativity, all Earth Grid negativity, all
        negative planetary mass consciousness, all violence, all
        hatred, and the negativity of all people forever.

    b) Ask for enlightenment.

    c) Ask for freedom forever from all Earth negativity, all Earth
        Grid negativity, all negative planetary mass consciousness, all
        violence, all hatred, and the negativity of all people. Ask for
        freedom from all restraints to your energy on all levels, and to
        your life and life path from these negative energies forever.

9. Remember to thank the Divine Director and the Lords of Karma
    with each request.

Process III Archangel Michael's Sword, Shield, and Chalice

ARCHANGEL MICHAEL IS THE PROTECTING ARCHANGEL OF THE EARTH. THE BLUE Ray of his Sword is used to fight evil and protect the Light, his Shield prevents old karma from returning to you, and his Chalice is for automatic self-healing. Additions to these protections will be given to you later.

This process is best done the last thing at night before sleep. You will feel movement in your energy from the installation and activation all night. In the morning, ask again if the Sword, Shield, and Chalice are fully installed and if they are activated. If they are not, repeat the request.

If you are bringing in a Goddess, ask that the Sword, Shield, and Chalice be installed in you, your Goddess, your union, total union, and ascension. They will be installed in different places. Make sure they are kept fully activated.

1. Ask to speak with Divine Director, the Lords of Karma, and Archangel Michael.

2. Ask if you may have ARCHANGEL MICHAEL'S SWORD of Truth and Protection installed in your energy. It is used to fight evil and protect the Light.

3. If the answer is "yes," ask where the Sword is to be installed.

4. When you know, do a complete Lords of Karma process requesting that the Sword of Archangel Michael be installed in your energy at the designated location on all levels and through all systems. It's time to pick up the Sword to protect life on Earth—ask for the ability and safety to do so.

5. Next, ask if you may have ARCHANGEL MICHAEL'S KARMIC SHIELD installed in your energy. It protects you from the return of old karma.

6. If the answer is "yes," ask where the Shield is to be installed.

7. Do a complete Lords of Karma process requesting that Archangel Michael's Karmic Shield be installed in your energy at the designated location on all levels and through all systems.

8. When this is done, ask if you may have ARCHANGEL MICHAEL'S CHALICE of Healing and Regeneration installed in your energy. Its use is for automatic energy healing.

9. If the answer is "yes," ask where the Chalice is to be installed.

10. When you know, do a complete Lords of Karma process requesting that the Chalice of Archangel Michael be installed in your energy at the designated location on all levels and through all systems.

11. Next, ask the Divine Director, the Lords of Karma, and Archangel Michael to fully activate the Sword, Shield, and Chalice immediately, continuously, irrevocably, and forever in your energy, through all the levels, components, and systems of your Be-ing. Ask for full insulation of your energy to protect the activations.

12. Clearly see yourself picking up the Sword. Ask for Archangel Michael's guidance as to when to do so and how to use it, and ask for his protection. Agree to use this Sword only to protect and defend the Light and the Goddess.

13. Do the full karmic process to finish. If you need to read it, you may do so from the previous processes.

14. Thank the Lords of Karma, Divine Director, and Archangel Michael.

Process IV   Divine Director and Other Planet Karma

WE HAVE HAD MANY MORE LIFETIMES ON OTHER PLANETS THAN WE HAVE HAD on Earth, and therefore will have much karma and many karmic contracts remaining from those lifetimes. This is Galactic Karma, and it may also accrue from events in between-life states. The following process addresses Galactic Karma specifically for the first time. Use it for everything in your life that remains to be healed, and for all requests until Process XI, the multidimensional Short Process. The canceling of other-planet (Galactic) karmic contracts will result in the closing of your Crown for about four hours for the reprogramming of your Galactic Creational Computers.

If you are bringing in a Goddess, make all requests for you, your Goddess, your union, total union, and ascension.

1. Ask to speak with Divine Director and the Lords of Karma.

2. Ask to CANCEL ALL KARMA AND ALL KARMIC CONTRACTS FROM EARTH AND ALL OTHER PLANETS AND BETWEEN THEM with (your request).

3. If the answer is "yes," ask for the healing:
   Fully, completely, permanently, and forever,
   Through all the levels and components of your Be-ing.
   Immediately and instantly.

4. If the answer is "yes," ask for the healing through your:
   Mind Grid level
   DNA level
   Karmic contract level
   All core soul levels and beyond
   All ascension levels
   All cellular and chromosomal levels
   All connections, channels, and pathways
   All systems

5. When all of these are "yes," ask for the healing:

> From beyond your Moment of Self to below and beyond the Center of the Earth and all planets,
>
> From below and beyond the Center of all planets to beyond your Moment of Self, and
>
> At your Moment of Self and your Creation.

6. Ask to seal the healing unto the Light and unto protection forever.

7. Ask for these healings:

> Through all the levels and all the bodies and between them,
>
> Through all the lifetimes on Earth and on all other planets and between them, including the present lifetime,
>
> Heal all the damage and end all negative effects,
>
> And bring the healing into the present NOW.

8. Thank Divine Director and the Lords of Karma.

Universal Healings Ask to cancel all karma and all karmic contracts from Earth and all other planets and between them with the following:

> a) The Negative Form in all of its manifestations
>
> b) All manifestations and sources of all evil
>
> c) All attacks upon your energy and Be-ing from all sources
>
> d) All energy damage from all sources and manifestations of all attacks and evil

Use this process for all unhealed karma with people and situations in your life that have not cleared with previous Lords of Karma requests. You may be made aware of many situations and lifetimes that require this clearing. These will be long-term, long-standing, serious situations that have remained in your energy and karma over many lifetimes.

Process V   Healing Core Soul Damage

THE PROCESS BELOW IS SELF-EXPLANATORY AND VERY IMPORTANT. I HAVE NEVER met anyone without core soul damage, and this request asks for its healing on Galactic levels that you have not reached before. If you are bringing in a Goddess, remember to ask for all requests for you, your Goddess, your union, total union, and ascension.

1. Ask to speak with Divine Director and the Lords of Karma.

2. Ask to CANCEL ALL KARMA AND ALL KARMIC CONTRACTS WITH CORE SOUL DAMAGE from all sources, from Earth and all other planets and between them. Ask to cancel all karma and all karmic contracts with the negative effects from this damage, and ask for complete healing.

3. Ask for the healing:
   > Fully, completely, permanently, and forever,
   > Through all the levels and components of your Be-ing and between them.
   > Immediately and instantly.

4. Ask for the healing through your:
   > Mind Grid level
   > DNA level
   > Karmic contract level
   > All core soul levels and beyond
   > All ascension levels
   > All cellular and chromosomal levels
   > All connections, channels, and pathways
   > All systems

5. Ask for the healing:

> From beyond your Moment of Self to below and beyond the Center of the Earth and all planets,
>
> From below and beyond the Center of all planets to beyond your Moment of Self, and
>
> At your Moment of Self and your Creation.

6. Ask to seal the healing unto the Light and unto protection forever.

7. Ask for the healing:

> Through all the levels and all the bodies and between them,
>
> Through all the lifetimes on Earth and on all other planets and between them, including the present lifetime,
>
> Heal all the damage and end all negative effects,
>
> And bring the healing into the present NOW.

8. Thank Divine Director and the Lords of Karma.

Universal Healings Repeat the above process with the following, asking each time to cancel all karma and all karmic contracts from Earth and all other planets and between them with each.

> a) Ask to cancel all karma and all karmic contracts with all DNA damage and negative mutation from all sources. Also ask for total clearing, healing, reconnection, and activation of your full complement of DNA strands.
>
> b) Ask that all positive encoding crystals of the Light be installed in your energy.
>
> c) Ask to cancel all karma and all karmic contracts with Mind Grid damage from all sources, and with all damage to your connections and interactions with the planetary Mind Grid.
>
> d) Ask to heal all your connections and interactions with all Planetary Grid structures on Earth and all other planets and between them.

e) Ask to cancel all karma and all karmic contracts with all damage to your Moment of Self through all the levels, components, and systems of your Be-ing.

f) Ask for total healing of your Soul Matrix.

g) Ask to cancel all karma and all karmic contracts with all that blocks and obstructs your life path.

You have made some of these requests before—to heal Earth karma; repeat them using this other-planet process for all galaxies. Remember to say thank you with each.

Process VI Healing Your Creation

EVERYONE HAS CREATIONAL DAMAGE—FROM EARTH, THE GALAXIES, AND ON ALL other levels. The further out into Galactic, Universal, and Cosmic healing you go, the more such damage you will find. If your request is denied, ask what is needed to release the "no." You may be shown other lifetimes, and there may be a series of requests you need to make. Completing this process will invoke a major healing. Repeat the request again later, using Short Process XI, when you have learned it. This begins a series of creational healings that continues through the remainder of *Essential Energy Balancing II.*

Once again as a reminder, if you are bringing in a Goddess, make all requests for you, your Goddess, your union, total union, and ascension. Your Goddess will not be exempt from creational damage, Galactic or on other levels. Your own damage is only a reflection of Hers.

1. Ask to speak with Divine Director and the Lords of Karma.

2. Ask to heal ALL THAT MAY HAVE GONE WRONG AT YOUR CREATION and its negative effects through all your lifetimes on Earth, on all other planets, and in all between-life states. Ask to cancel immediately and instantly all karma and karmic contracts with all damage and its sources, and with all that may have gone wrong at your separation from the Light.

3. Ask for the healing:
      Fully, completely, permanently, and forever,
      Through all the levels and components of your Be-ing and
         between them,
      Immediately and instantly.

4. Ask for the healing through your:
      Mind Grid level
      DNA level

Karmic contract level

All core soul levels and beyond

All ascension levels

All cellular and chromosomal levels

All connections, channels, and pathways

All systems

And between all of these

5. Ask for the healing:

From beyond your Moment of Self to below and beyond the
Center of the Earth and all planets,

From below and beyond the Center of the Earth and all planets to beyond your Moment of Self, and

At your Moment of Self and your Creation.

6. Ask to seal the healing unto the Light and unto protection forever.

7. Ask for this healing:

Through all the levels and all the bodies and between them,

Through all the lifetimes on Earth and on all other planets and
between them, including the present lifetime,

Heal all the damage and end all negative effects,

And bring the healing into the present NOW.

8. Thank Divine Director and the Lords of Karma.

Process VII   Energy Protection

THE FOLLOWING PROCESSES CONTINUE THE INTENT OF TOTAL ENERGY protection and protection from all evil. They also heal any remaining damage from negative interference to your energy. They continue and support the protection and regeneration offered by Archangel Michael's Sword, Shield, and Chalice. When you learn Process XI, repeat these requests using the advanced process. In *Essential Energy Balancing III,* you will be able to make the requests below complete.

If you are bringing in a Goddess, remember to make these requests for you, your Goddess, your union, total union, and ascension. Your Goddess needs these protections as much as you do, if not more.

1. Ask to speak with Divine Director and the Lords of Karma.

2. Ask to make your energy—on Earth, on all other planets, and between them—a SELF-PROTECTING, SELF-DEFENDING, SELF-CLEARING, SELF-REPAIRING, AND SELF-HEALING MECHANISM through all the levels, components, and systems of your Be-ing and between them. Ask to cancel immediately and instantly all karma and all karmic contracts—from Earth and from all other planets and between them—that may be preventing these requests. Ask that Archangel Michael's Sword, Shield, and Chalice encompass these requests through all the levels, components, and systems of your Be-ing and between them.

3. Ask for these healings:
   Fully, completely, permanently, and forever,
   Through all the levels and components of your Be-ing and
      between them
   Immediately and instantly.

4. Ask for these healings through your:
   Mind Grid level
   DNA level

Karmic contract level

All core soul levels and beyond

All ascension levels

All cellular and chromosomal levels

All connections, channels, and pathways

All systems

And between all of these

5. Ask for these healings:

From beyond your Moment of Self to below and beyond the Center of the Earth and all planets,

From below and beyond the Center of all planets to beyond your Moment of Self, and

At your Moment of Self and your Creation.

6. Seal the healing unto the Light and unto protection forever.

7. Ask for these healings:

Through all the levels and all the bodies and between them,

Through all the lifetimes on Earth and on all other planets and between them, including the present lifetime,

Heal all the damage and end all negative effects,

And bring the healing into the present NOW.

8. If all is "yes," this portion of the process is complete. Go to the Universal Healings to continue it. Thank Divine Director and the Lords of Karma before going on.

Universal Healings These are necessary to complete the work begun above.

a) Ask to make your energy invulnerable to all sources and manifestations of all evil, all energy attacks, all harm, all negative interference, and all energy damage through all the levels and components of your Be-ing, including all connections. Ask to cancel immediately and instantly all karma and all karmic contracts from Earth, all other planets, and between them preventing this healing. Complete the process as above.

b) Ask for total energy protection and total activation of all energy protection through all the levels and components of your Be-ing and between them, through all lifetimes on Earth and on all other planets and between them. Ask to cancel immediately and instantly all karma and all karmic contracts from Earth, all other planets, and between them preventing your full protection.

c) Ask to raise and strengthen your Light and energy vibration to be so strong that no evil can enter, remain, or exist in your energy or ever approach it. Ask to cancel immediately and instantly all karma and all karmic contracts from Earth, all other planets and between them preventing this healing. Complete the full process.

d) Ask for full healing of your physical body from all manifestations and sources of all evil, all energy attacks, all harm, all negative interference, and all energy damage. Go through the full karmic clearing process above with each of these requests.

Remember to thank Divine Director and the Lords of Karma after each request and to have gratitude in all things.

Process VIII   Annihilation of All Evil

THE PROCESS BELOW ASKS FOR THE CLEARING OF YOUR ENERGY FROM ALL negative interference and evil, and then extends that clearing to throughout the oneness of the All. This is the first of many such requests.

If you are bringing in a Goddess, remember to ask for all requests for you, your Goddess, your union, total union, and ascension.

1. Ask to speak with Divine Director, the Lords of Karma, the Karmic Board, and Archangels Michael and Ashtar.

2. Ask to ANNIHILATE, EXTINGUISH, UNCREATE, AND OBLITERATE ALL THAT IS EVIL FROM YOUR ENERGY AND FROM THE EARTH FOREVER, from all manifestations and sources on Earth, all other planets and between them, and from all lifetimes. Ask also to annihilate, extinguish, uncreate, and obliterate all negative interference and negative effects from all sources and manifestations of evil from your energy and from the Earth forever.

3. Ask to annihilate, extinguish, uncreate, and obliterate these evils from yourself and from the Earth through:

    All the levels and components of your Be-ing, the Earth's Be-ing and between them,

    Fully, completely, permanently, and forever,

    Immediately and instantly.

4. Ask to annihilate, extinguish, uncreate, and obliterate these evils from yourself and from the Earth through the:

    Mind Grid level

    DNA level

    Karmic contract level

    All core soul levels and beyond

    All ascension levels

    All chromosomal and cellular levels

    All connections, channels, and pathways

All systems,

And between them

5. Ask for these for yourself and the Earth:

From beyond yours and the Earth's Moment of Self to below and beyond the Center of the Earth and all planets,

From below and beyond the Center of the Earth and all planets to beyond yours and the Earth's Moment of Self, and

At yours and the Earth's Moment of Self and Creation.

6. Ask to seal the cleared, healed energy unto the Light and unto protection forever for you and for the Earth.

7. Ask for these healings for you and for the Earth:

Through all the levels, all the bodies and between them,

Through all lifetimes on Earth and on all other planets and between them,

Heal all the damage and end all negative effects from you and from the Earth,

And bring the healing into the present NOW.

8. Ask to annihilate, extinguish, uncreate, and obliterate all sources and manifestations of evil from the list below. You may do the list all at once.

All components, connections, and systems of your energy

All Planetary Grids, structures, and connections

All components of the Earth's energy

All Be-ings on the Earth, human or otherwise, alive or otherwise, and all multidimensional Be-ings

Our Moon and all moons

Our Solar System and all solar systems

Our Galaxy and all galaxies

Our Universe and all universes

All planets, worlds, and between the worlds

All dimensions and between them

All dimensional accesses and between them

> Our Cosmos and all cosmos
> And beyond, and everything in between

9. Ask for these healings immediately and instantly, past, present, and future, forever and NOW.

10. Remember to thank the Lords of Karma, Divine Director, the Karmic Board, and Archangels Michael and Ashtar.

Process IX Multidimensional Karmic Release

WE ARE MULTIDIMENSIONAL BE-INGS, EXISTING IN MANY DIMENSIONS AND realities at once, as well as having had existences on many planets besides the Earth and the Earth physical plane. There are many states of existence and systems of Be-ing besides our own. This process addresses all karma and all karmic contracts that resist total release with any other method. Use this for all difficulties still remaining in your life after all the other processes are completed, and repeat previous requests using this process as needed. The arbitrator of multidimensional karma is Divine Director. The first example is for healing all obstructions to your life's work.

This process and the one that follows it are involved and complicated, but with Process X they will be complete and will not be needed again. Use them by reading them from the book; there is no need to memorize them. With Process XI, things get much simpler. It is necessary at this time to do these long and wordy formats as crucial reprogrammings of your Galactic Creational Computers. Once again, if you are bringing in a Goddess, make all requests for you, your Goddess, your union, total union, and ascension.

1. Ask to speak with the Lords of Karma and Divine Director.

2. Ask to cancel immediately and instantly all karma and karmic contracts from Earth and all other planets and between them, from all lifetimes and between them, with ALL OBSTRUCTIONS AND THEIR SOURCES TO YOUR LIFE PURPOSE, LIFE WORK, AND LIFE PATH through all multidimensions and between them, of and between all dimensions of your multidimensional Be-ing.

3. Ask for the healing:
   Fully, completely, permanently, and forever,
   Through all the levels and components of your multi-
   dimensional Be-ing and between them,
   Immediately and instantly.

4. When you receive a "yes," ask for the healing through all multi-
    dimensions and between them, of and between all dimensions of
    your multidimensional Be-ing through your:
    > Mind Grid level
    > DNA level
    > Karmic contract level
    > All core soul levels and beyond
    > All ascension levels
    > All cellular and chromosomal levels
    > All connections, channels, and pathways
    > All systems
    > And between them

5. Ask for the healing:
    > From beyond your multidimensional Moment of Self and
    > multidimensional Creation to below the Center of the Earth
    > and all planets, including all planetary structures and grid
    > structures, the Earth Grid, and all connections and interac-
    > tions, through all multidimensions and between them, of and
    > between all dimensions of your multidimensional Be-ing.

6. Ask for the healing:
    > At your multidimensional Moment of Self and multi-
    > dimensional Creation, through all multidimensions and
    > between them, of and between all dimensions of your multi-
    > dimensional Be-ing.

7. Ask to seal the healing unto the Light and unto protection forever
    through all multidimensions and between them, of and between
    all dimensions of your multidimensional Be-ing.

8. Ask for the healing (getting a "yes" with each step):
    > Through all the levels and all the bodies of your multi-
    > dimensional Be-ing and between them,
    > Through all the lifetimes on Earth and on all other planets and
    > between all lifetimes, including the present lifetime,

through all multidimensions and between them, of and between all dimensions of your multidimensional Be-ing,

Through all dimensions, dimensional states, dimensional structures, multidimensions and between them of your multidimensional Be-ing,

Through all multidimensional existences, existence states, existence structures and between them, through all multidimensions and your multidimensional Be-ing,

Through all multidimensional realities, alternate realities, simultaneous realities, multiple realities, and between them, through all multidimensions of your multidimensional Be-ing,

Through all multidimensional lifetimes, alternate lifetimes, simultaneous lifetimes, multiple lifetimes and between them, through all multidimensions of your multidimensional Be-ing,

Heal all the damage and end all negative effects through all multidimensions and between them, of and between all dimensions of your multidimensional Be-ing,

And bring the healing into the present NOW, immediately and instantly, through all multidimensions and between them, of and between all dimensions of your multidimensional Be-ing.

Past, present, and future,

Forever.

NOW.

9. Say thank you.

Universal Healings

a) Repeating and adding to Process II, ask to raise your Light beyond the negative mass consciousness of Earth and all other planets.

b) Repeat Processes V and VI to continue to heal all core soul damage using this method. It is extremely important to do this.

c) Using the wording of this process, ask for shielding and protection from all evil and negativity coming to you through the planetary structures, grid structures, Earth Grid, the core of the Earth, and all planetary interactions and connections. Ask for protection from all Earth Change planetary shifts, and request total healing of all damage from all of these.

d) Repeat any other requests you feel need extending through the dimensions.

Proceed to Process X.

Process X Multidimensional All-Healing

THIS LONG PROCESS CONTINUES THE WORK OF PROCESS IX. IT IS THE LAST TIME you will do a process so involved. If you are bringing in a Goddess, remember to ask for all requests for you, your Goddess, your union, total union, and ascension. Evil and negative interference were done first to them, to replicate and continue in us and in all of life.

1. Ask to speak with the Lords of Karma and Divine Director.

2. Ask to cancel and end immediately and instantly all karma and karmic contracts from Earth and all other planets and between them, from all lifetimes and between them, with THE SOURCE OF ALL EVIL AND ALL OF ITS CREATIONS AND MANIFESTA-TIONS through all multidimensions and between them of your multidimensional Be-ing.

3. Ask for the healing:
    Fully, completely, permanently, and forever,
    Through all the levels and components of your multi-
        dimensional Be-ing and between them,
    Immediately and instantly.

4. Ask for the healing through all multidimensions and between them of your multidimensional Be-ing through your:
    Mind Grid level
    DNA level
    Karmic contract level
    All core soul levels and beyond
    All ascension levels
    All cellular and chromosomal levels
    All connections, channels, and pathways
    All systems
    And between them

5. When you receive a "yes," ask for the healing:

   From beyond your multidimensional Moment of Self and multidimensional Creation to below the Center of the Earth and all planets, including all planetary structures and grid structures, the Earth Grid, and all connections and interactions; through all multidimensions and between them of your multidimensional Be-ing.

6. Ask for the healing:

   At your multidimensional Moment of Self and multidimensional Creation, through all multidimensions and between them of your multidimensional Be-ing.

7. Ask to seal the healing unto the Light and unto protection forever through all multidimensions and between them of your multidimensional Be-ing.

8. Ask for the healing (getting a "yes" with each step):

   Through all the levels and all the bodies of your multidimensional Be-ing and between them,

   Through all the lifetimes on Earth and on all other planets and between all lifetimes, including the present lifetime, through all multidimensions and between them of your multidimensional Be-ing,

   Through all dimensions, dimensional states, dimensional structures, multidimensions and between them and your multidimensional Be-ing,

   Through all multidimensional existences, existence states, existence structures and between them, through all multidimensions and your multidimensional Be-ing,

   Through all multidimensional realities, alternate realities, simultaneous realities, multiple realities and between them, through all multidimensions of your multidimensional Be-ing,

Through all multidimensional lifetimes, alternate lifetimes, simultaneous lifetimes, multiple lifetimes and between them, through all multidimensions of your multidimensional Be-ing,

Heal all the damage and end all negative effects through all multidimensions and between them of your multidimensional Be-ing,

And bring the healing into the present NOW, immediately and instantly, through all multidimensions and between them of your multidimensional Be-ing,

Past, present, and future,

Forever.

NOW.

9. Say thank you.

Universal Healing

a) Repeat this process in the format above, with the request worded to read "all sources and manifestations of all evil."

Process XI   Short Process

THIS IS THE ABBREVIATED VERSION OF PROCESS IX AND PROCESS X. YOU WILL USE
it for many requests and may wish to memorize it. Ask your question, taking it through the steps below. When you have a "yes" for all portions of
the request, ask if you need to go further. If not, the process is finished; if
yes, you must do the long version to attain your full request, by continuing the process to completion (Processes IX and X, steps 4 through 9).
Few requests will now require the long process.

The sample requests below are important to complete, but are not the
only things you will ask for. Use the precise wording and format. As with
every process, if you are bringing in a Goddess, you must make all
requests for you, your Goddess, your union, total union, and ascension.

1. Ask to speak with Divine Director, the Lords of Karma, and the
    Karmic Board.

2. Ask them to cancel all karma and all karmic contracts from all
    sources with SEPARATION FROM SPIRIT. Ask for the full mani-
    festation of your total union with Spirit:

    > on Earth and all other planets and between them, through all
    > lifetimes and between them, through all dimensions and
    > multidimensions and between them, of and between all
    > dimensions of your multidimensional Be-ing.

3. Ask for the healing:

    > Fully, completely, permanently, and forever,
    > Through all levels and components of your Be-ing, all connec-
    >   tions, all dimensions, all systems and between them of, and
    >   between all dimensions of your multidimensional Be-ing,
    > Immediately and instantly,
    > Past, present, future,
    > NOW.

4. When you receive a "yes" to this point, ask if you need to continue the process. If the answer is "no," the request is granted and the process is finished. If the answer is "yes," continue and complete the full request.

5. Thank the Lords of Karma, Divine Director, and the Karmic Board.

Universal Healings These are important to complete. If they cannot be granted with the short format, take them through the full extended process.

a) Ask to heal your ability for Spirit to work through you. Ask to cancel all karma and all karmic contracts, and so on that prevent it.

b) Ask for the healing of all energy connections of all types, and to cancel all karma and all karmic contracts of energy damage or disconnection. Use the wording and format above.

c) Ask for healing from all the negative effects of evil of all types and from all sources on your energy and life.

d) Ask to heal all damage to your psychic abilities and all their components, connections, and systems.

Process XII   Karmic Dispensation

THIS IS A REQUEST FOR THE RELEASE AND COMPLETION OF EARTH OR GALACTIC Karma, not through your understanding and resolution of the issue, but through Karmic Mercy. These releases are gifts from Divine Director or Nada. Use this process for all issues that seem to have no answer and that have been resistant to all previous karmic work and requests. No matter what you have done or asked for, these are the issues that still remain. Try the following to solve them. Karmic Dispensation will not be given for every request you make for it; it is a special gift, to be taken seriously and with gratitude.

As with all other requests, if you are bringing in a Goddess, ask for it for you, your Goddess, your union, total union, and ascension.

1. Ask to speak with Divine Director, Nada, the Lords of Karma, and the Karmic Board.

2. Ask for FULL KARMIC DISPENSATION AND RELEASE FROM *(your request),* from Earth and all other planets and between them, from all lifetimes and between them, and from all sources, through all multidimensions and between them of your multi-dimensional Be-ing.

3. If you get a "yes," do the Short Process (Process XI). If, at the end of that, you are told there is no need to go further, the issue is resolved. If you need to go on, complete the long form (Process IX).

4. If you get a "no," ask what you need to see, know, or do to have the full release. There may be an unresolved past life or karmic pattern, often with an other-planetary lifetime source. The source may be core soul damage or other damage from between lifetimes. You may be given other directions as well. Follow them. Ask to clear the source you are shown, using the short or long process,

then repeat your request. Sometimes rewording the request also resolves a "no."

5. Often the request for Karmic Dispensation is enough. You will be told that there is no need to go through any further process than to ask for the release.

6. Thank Divine Director, Nada, the Lords of Karma, and the Karmic Board. Karmic dispensation is the greatest of gifts.

Process XIII Karmic Renewal

WE HAVE ASKED TO CANCEL A MULTITUDE OF NEGATIVE KARMAS AND KARMIC contracts. This process is to reinstate the positive karmas we were created to have as our birthright for our lifetimes on Earth and on all other planets. Ask for these carefully and precisely, as you will receive what is granted—and have to live with it. The requests must be for the good of all; no request that harms you, anyone else, or the planet will be granted.

This is a chance to have the things you want for your life. Too many people, especially women, are afraid to make requests to benefit themselves. Overcome this inhibition, and ask for what you want and need.

If you are bringing in a Goddess, make all requests for you, your Goddess, your union, total union, and ascension.

1. Ask to speak with Divine Director, Nada, the Lords of Karma, and the Karmic Board.

2. Request to CREATE KARMIC RENEWAL FOR ALL THE GIFTS THAT HAVE BEEN WITHDRAWN FROM YOU OR LOST TO YOU from all sources and for all reasons.

3. Ask to CREATE KARMIC RENEWAL FOR HARMONY IN YOUR LIFE AND RELATIONSHIPS, on Earth and all other planets and between them, for this lifetime, all lifetimes and between them, through all multidimensions and between them of your multidimensional Be-ing.

4. If the request is granted, ask for the healing:
   Fully, completely, permanently, and forever,
   Through all levels, components, connections, systems, dimensions, and between them of your multidimensional Be-ing,
   Immediately and instantly.

5. When you receive a "yes" to the above, ask if you need to continue the process. If the answer is "no," the request is granted and

the process is finished. If the answer is "yes," continue and complete the full request using the long process (Processes IX and X, steps 4 through 9).

6. Thank the Lords of Karma, Nada, Divine Director, and the Karmic Board.

Universal Healings Use the exact wording of the process above and individualize the following requests:

a) Request anything and everything that you feel to be missing in your life.

b) Ask for a sense of purpose in your life.

c) Ask to create Karmic Renewal for inner peace, inner calm, inner certainty, and inner guidance.

d) Request the creation of Karmic Renewal for positive self-image and self-love.

e) Ask to create Karmic Renewal for a healthy body, emotions, mind, and spirit. Request to cancel all karma and all karmic contracts with all physical dis-eases or conditions you may have. If you have been refused Karmic Renewal, these contracts may need to be canceled first.

f) Request to create Karmic Renewal for easy prosperity and abundance. If there is a "no" with this, you may find that there is negative karma or karmic contracts to cancel first. Find and release them. These contracts may not be from Earth lifetimes but from lifetimes on other planets.

g) Ask to create Karmic Renewal for the full manifestation of the Light in your life.

Process XIV   Sealing Against All Evil

THIS SERIES OF REQUESTS SEALS YOUR ENERGY TO PREVENT EVIL FROM HARMING you or working through you—forever. Use the Short Process for the following, and keep the wording of your requests exactly as I have written them. Ask at the end if you need to continue through the long format. (The Short Process is usually all that is needed.) The basic request with a complete Short Process is given below in the first example, and a series of additional requests follows it. All the requests are necessary. Note that sealing may cause your Crown to be closed for repatterning for up to twenty-four hours.

The requests below include you, your Goddess, your union, total union, and ascension, whether or not you are bringing in a Goddess.

1. Ask Divine Director, the Lords of Karma, and the Karmic Board to SEAL YOUR ENERGY AND ALL ENERGY COMPONENTS, CONNECTIONS, AND SYSTEMS AGAINST THE SOURCE OF ALL EVIL AND ALL ITS CREATIONS AND MANIFESTATIONS FOREVER. Ask to SEAL YOUR ENERGY AND ALL ENERGY COMPONENTS, CONNECTIONS, AND SYSTEMS FOR THE LIGHT FOREVER and to SEAL YOUR ENERGY AND ALL ENERGY COMPONENTS, CONNECTIONS, AND SYSTEMS UNTO THE LIGHT AND UNTO PROTECTION FOREVER.

    Ask that all damage be healed, and that all components too damaged to heal be fully replaced in accordance with the Light. Request to annihilate, extinguish, uncreate, obliterate, and remove all negative effects, and to end all access by the Source of All Evil and its creations and manifestations to your energy forever. Do these as one request.

2. Ask that all karma and all karmic contracts with the Source of All Evil and all its creations and manifestations, and all karma and karmic contracts preventing the sealing against these, be canceled

immediately and forever. Ask for these healings from Earth and all other planets and between them, all lifetimes and between them, through all multidimensions and between them, of and between all dimensions of your multidimensional Be-ing.

3. Ask for these healings for you, your Goddess, your union, total union, and ascension. Ask that these healings include all energy connections and interactions with the above, and with all sources of the Light, with all connections and interactions with the Earth and all planets, and with the Well of Life and Fire of Life at the Center of all planets. Ask for these through all multidimensions and between them, of and between all dimensions of your multidimensional Be-ing.

4. Ask for these healings fully, completely, permanently, and forever, through all the levels and components of your Be-ing, through all dimensions, all connections, all systems and between them, through all multidimensions and between them, of and between all dimensions of your multidimensional Be-ing.

5. Ask for these healings immediately and instantly, past, present, and future, forever and NOW.

6. Thank the Divine Director, the Lords of Karma, and the Karmic Board. This completes the first request.

7. Repeat the above process for each of the following requests. It is important to do all of them.
    a) Ask to CLEAR, HEAL, RECONNECT, AND SEAL AGAINST THE SOURCE OF ALL EVIL AND ALL ITS CREATIONS AND MANIFESTATIONS FOREVER YOUR CONNEC-TIONS TO THE WELL OF LIFE AND FIRE OF LIFE AT THE CENTER OF THE EARTH. Seal them for the Light for-ever, and unto the Light and unto protection forever.
    b) Request to SEAL AGAINST THE SOURCE OF ALL EVIL AND ALL ITS CREATIONS AND MANIFESTATIONS

FOREVER ALL YOUR PLANETARY CONNECTIONS AND INTERACTIONS; seal them for the Light forever, and unto the Light and unto protection forever.

c) Ask to SEAL AGAINST THE SOURCE OF ALL EVIL AND ALL ITS CREATIONS AND MANIFESTATIONS FOREVER YOUR CONNECTIONS AND INTERACTIONS WITH: YOUR GODDESS, NADA, LIGHT MOTHER, THE SHEK-INAH, THE RADIANCE OF THE LIGHT BEYOND THE GODDESS, ALL CREATION, THE PURE LIGHT BEYOND CREATION, ALL SOURCES OF THE LIGHT, THE SHEK-INAH'S LIGHT—AND BETWEEN THEM. Ask to seal these connections and interactions for the Light forever, and unto the Light and unto protection forever.

d) Ask to SEAL YOUR CREATION ON ALL LEVELS AGAINST THE SOURCE OF ALL EVIL AND ALL ITS CREATIONS AND MANIFESTATIONS FOREVER, for the Light forever, and unto the Light and unto protection forever.

e) Ask to SEAL YOUR MOMENT OF SELF AND ALL ITS COMPONENTS AGAINST THE SOURCE OF ALL EVIL AND ALL ITS CREATIONS AND MANIFESTATIONS FOREVER, for the Light forever, and unto the Light and unto protection forever.

f) Request to SEAL YOUR DNA AND ALL CHROMOSOMAL AND CELLULAR SYSTEMS AND BETWEEN THEM AGAINST THE SOURCE OF ALL EVIL AND ALL ITS CREATIONS AND MANIFESTATIONS FOREVER. Ask to seal them for the Light forever, and unto the Light and unto protection forever.

g) Ask to SEAL YOUR GROUNDING SYSTEM AND ALL ITS LEVELS, COMPONENTS, AND CONNECTIONS, AGAINST THE SOURCE OF ALL EVIL AND ALL ITS CREATIONS AND MANIFESTATIONS FOREVER. Seal them for the Light forever, and unto the Light and unto protection forever.

h) Request the SEALING OF YOUR MIND GRID, AND ALL ITS COMPONENTS, CONNECTIONS AND SYSTEMS ON ALL LEVELS, AGAINST THE SOURCE OF ALL EVIL AND ALL ITS CREATIONS AND MANIFESTATIONS FOREVER. Ask to seal them for the Light forever, and unto the Light and unto protection forever.

i) Ask to SEAL YOUR CROWN CHAKRA, CROWN CHAKRA COMPLEX, UNIFIED CROWN, AND ALL CROWN SYSTEMS AGAINST THE SOURCE OF ALL EVIL AND ALL ITS CREATIONS AND MANIFESTATIONS FOREVER. Ask to seal them for the Light forever, and unto the Light and unto protection forever.

j) Request to SEAL ALL CHAKRAS, CHAKRA COMPLEXES, UNIFIED CHAKRAS, AND ALL CHAKRA SYSTEMS AGAINST THE SOURCE OF ALL EVIL AND ALL ITS CREATIONS AND MANIFESTATIONS FOREVER. Ask to seal them for the Light forever, and unto the Light and unto protection forever.

k) Ask to SEAL YOUR AURA AND ALL COMPONENTS AND CONNECTIONS OF YOUR AURA THROUGH ALL LEVELS, BODIES, AND SYSTEMS AGAINST THE SOURCE OF ALL EVIL AND ALL ITS CREATIONS AND MANIFESTATIONS FOREVER. Request to seal them for the Light forever, and unto the Light and unto protection forever.

l) Ask to SEAL ALL COMMUNICATION AND RECEPTION SYSTEMS AND THEIR CONNECTIONS AND COMPONENTS AGAINST THE SOURCE OF ALL EVIL AND ALL ITS CREATIONS AND MANIFESTATIONS FOREVER, for the Light forever, and unto the Light and unto protection forever.

m) Request the SEALING OF YOUR ASCENSION AND ALL ASCENSION COMPONENTS, CONNECTIONS, SYSTEMS AND BETWEEN THEM AGAINST THE SOURCE OF ALL EVIL AND ALL ITS CREATIONS AND MANIFESTATIONS FOREVER. Ask to seal them for the Light forever, and unto the Light and unto protection forever.

n) Ask to SEAL YOUR ENTIRE TUBE OF LIGHT AND CRYSTAL SHAFT THROUGH ALL COMPONENTS, CONNECTIONS, AND SYSTEMS AGAINST THE SOURCE OF ALL EVIL AND ALL ITS CREATIONS AND MANIFESTATIONS FOREVER, for the Light forever, and unto the Light and unto protection forever.

o) Ask to SEAL YOUR I-AM PRESENCE AGAINST THE SOURCE OF ALL EVIL AND ALL ITS CREATIONS AND MANIFESTATIONS FOREVER, for the Light forever, and unto the Light and unto protection forever.

Your I-AM Presence is your Goddess, and this is the most important request of all.

Always thank Divine Director, the Lords of Karma, and the Karmic Board with each request.

Process XV   Annihilation of Evil: Extended Process

THE FOLLOWING SERIES OF REQUESTS USES THE SHORT PROCESS IN A FOUR-PART format. For each request, the steps ask to: (a) annihilate, extinguish, uncreate, and obliterate all evil; (b) cancel all karma and all karmic contracts with evil; (c) heal all the damage from evil; and (d) seal your energy against all evil forever. This is more precise and more complete than previous formats, and several requests using it are made here. It is important to do all the parts. The attacks referred to may be physical or otherwise, from all lifetimes on all planets, and from all between life states.

If you are bringing in a Goddess, as always, make all requests for you, your Goddess, your union, total union, and ascension.

1. Request to speak with Divine Director, the Lords of Karma, and the Karmic Board.

2. Ask to ANNIHILATE, EXTINGUISH, UNCREATE, AND OBLITERATE from your energy and all systems forever ALL ATTACKS AND ALL DAMAGE FROM ATTACKS FROM ALL SOURCES, including all creations and manifestations of the Source of All Evil. Ask for these from Earth and all other planets and between them, all lifetimes and between them, all dimensions and between them, and through all multidimensions and between them of your multidimensional Be-ing.

3. Request to cancel forever ALL KARMA AND ALL KARMIC CONTRACTS with all attacks and all damage from attacks from all sources, including all creations and manifestations of the Source of All Evil. Ask for these from Earth and all other planets and between them, all lifetimes and between them, all dimensions and between them, through all multidimensions and between them of your multidimensional Be-ing.

4. Request to HEAL ALL DAMAGE from all attacks from all sources, including from all creations and manifestations of the Source of

All Evil. Ask to replace all components, connections, and systems that are too damaged to be easily healed, in accordance with the Light. Request to remove all blockages, obstructions, and negative programming, to end all access by evil and all negative effects, and to remove and end all negative symbols and negative interference of all types. Ask to fully reconnect all connections and components, and to bring all systems back to full and optimal function with total safety and protection.

Ask for these from Earth and all other planets and between them, through all lifetimes and between them, all dimensions and between them, and through all multidimensions and between them, of and between all dimensions of your multidimensional Be-ing.

5. Make the request to SEAL YOUR ENERGY and all components, connections, and systems, and between them, forever against all attacks and damage from attacks from all sources, including all creations and manifestations of the Source of All Evil, and all the evils listed above. Request to seal your energy and all systems for the Light, and unto the Light and unto protection forever. Ask to cancel all karma and all karmic contracts preventing this total sealing.

Request these things from Earth and all other planets and between them, through all lifetimes and between them, all dimensions and between them, and through all multidimensions and between them, of and between all dimensions of your multidimensional Be-ing.

6. Repeat Steps 1 through 4 in the format above for ALL NEGATIVE INTERFERENCE OF ALL TYPES AND FROM ALL SOURCES, including all creations and manifestations of the Source of All Evil.

7. Repeat Steps 1 through 4 in the format above for ALL ALIEN ATTACKS AND INTERFERENCE from all planets and all sources,

including from all creations and manifestations of the Source of All Evil on all planets.

8. Repeat Steps 1 through 4 in the format above to END ALL ACCESS TO YOUR ENERGY BY EVIL from all sources and all manifestations, including all creations and manifestations of the Source of All Evil.

9. Make these requests for ALL BE-INGS and all the Light, for all Goddesses, all Goddess unions, all ascension Be-ings, and for all life—human and otherwise, incarnate and discarnate—on Earth and all other planets, through all lifetimes and dimensions and between them, of and between all multidimensional Be-ings. (Do Steps 1 through 4.)

10. Make these requests for YOUR GODDESS, whether you are bringing your Goddess into your energy or not. If you are bringing in your Goddess, the request is for you, your Goddess, your union, total union, and ascension.

11. Make these requests in the wording above for your HOME, BUSINESS, GARDEN AND LAND, CAR, ALL POSSESSIONS AND BELONGINGS, and for your FAMILY, MATE, CHILDREN, AND PETS.

12. Using this process, repeat your request to SEAL YOUR I-AM PRESENCE AGAINST ALL EVIL. It is important to do this.

13. Thank Divine Director, the Lords of Karma, and the Karmic Board at the completion of each request.

Process XVI   Healing Dis-Ease

HEALING DIS-EASE IS THE FIRST THING THAT COMES TO MIND FOR MOST PEOPLE regarding karma. This is an extended process for healing dis-eases and conditions. If you are bringing in a Goddess, make the request for you, your Goddess, your union, total union, and ascension.

1. Request the Lords of Karma, Divine Director, and the Karmic Board to REMOVE FROM YOUR DNA ALL DIS-EASE AND NEG-ATIVE PHYSICAL, EMOTIONAL, MENTAL, AND SPIRITUAL DIS-EASES AND CONDITIONS, immediately and instantly. Ask to cancel immediately and instantly all karma and all karmic contracts, and all vows given or received, with regard to all dis-eases and negative conditions from all sources, from Earth and all other planets and between them, all lifetimes and between them, through all dimensions and multidimensions and between them of your multidimensional Be-ing.

2. Ask to seal your DNA against all dis-ease, and against all negative physical, emotional, mental, and spiritual conditions forever, seal it for the Light forever, and unto the Light and unto protection forever. Request these sealings from Earth and all other planets and between them, all lifetimes and between them, through all dimensions and multidimensions and between them of your multidimensional Be-ing.

3. Ask for these healings fully, completely, permanently, and forever, through all the levels and components of your Be-ing, through all dimensions, all connections, all systems and between them, through all multidimensions and between them of your multi-dimensional Be-ing.

4. Ask for these healings immediately and instantly, past, present, and future, forever and NOW.

5. Thank the Lords of Karma, Divine Director, and the Karmic Board.

Universal Healings

a) Use this format to request removal of all cancer, stroke, and heart dis-ease from your DNA and karma/karmic contracts, as well as all artery dis-ease, hormone, and endocrine dis-ease, and all dis-eases related to stress. Do these as one process.

b) Use this format to request removal of all personal dis-eases and conditions from your DNA and karma/karmic contracts.

c) Repeat the process for any dis-eases that are generational and family-inherited karma. For example, if you had three grandparents with diabetes, ask to remove all diabetes from your DNA and your karma/karmic contracts.

d) Use this format and process for any dis-eases you fear.

e) Repeat this process asking that these dis-eases, and all dis-eases and negative physical, emotional, mental, and spiritual dis-eases and conditions, be removed from the planet and from all life on all planets forever.

Process XVII   Connecting with the Light

THE GALACTIC CORD IS YOUR PERSONAL PART OF THE CHAIN OF LIGHT THAT begins with the Shekinah at the creation of your soul and connects with your body through your Moment of Self into all heart systems. From the heart down, the Galactic Cord becomes the Grounding Cord, continuing to and through the Well of Life and Fire of Life at the Center of the Earth and all planets. In *Essential Energy Balancing,* I used the phrase "from beyond the Moment of Self to below the Center of the Earth" to incorporate all energy. In *Essential Energy Balancing II,* the more complete phrase is "from beyond the Pure Light above Creation to below the Well of Life and Fire of Life at the Center of the Earth and all planets and beyond."

This great central channel is subject to damage and disconnection. Few people are fully connected to all the sources of the Light—the connections via the Galactic Cord have been cut or disconnected over many incarnations, or the transformer templates have been damaged. The following process serves to heal all damage to the Galactic Cord and to reconnect you fully with the Light.

If you are bringing in a Goddess, be sure to make these requests for you, your Goddess, your union, total union, and ascension.

1. Ask to speak with Divine Director, the Lords of Karma, and the Karmic Board.

2. Request COMPLETE HEALING, REGENERATION, AND TOTAL RECONNECTION OF YOUR GALACTIC CORD SYSTEM through all the levels, components, connections, and systems of your Be-ing, from beyond the Pure Light above Creation to below the Well of Life and Fire of Life at the Center of the Earth and all planets and beyond, and everything in between. Ask to replace any components too damaged to easily heal and to bring all connections, components, and systems back to full and optimal func-

tion and perfection with total safety and protection forever. Ask for this also for all Chain of Light and Galactic Cord energy transformers—the Ascension Portal, Entrance Point, Galactic Connection Point, Earth Portal, and all others.

3. Ask for this healing through ALL CONNECTIONS AND INTERACTIONS WITH ALL SOURCES OF THE LIGHT: with the Ascended Masters, the Lords of Karma, the Karmic Board, Divine Director, the angels and archangels of the Light, all the Goddesses, Brede (our Great Goddess), Nada (our Great Mother), Demeter (our Earth Mother), Light Mother (our All-Mother), the Shekinah (our Great Cosmic Mother), the Radiance of the Light Beyond the Goddess, all Creation, and the Pure Light beyond, through all systems and between them.

4. Request this healing through ALL CONNECTIONS AND INTERACTIONS WITH THE EARTH AND ALL PLANETS: with and through all planetary systems, all Planetary Grids and grid structures, and the Well of Life and Fire of Life at the Center of the Earth and all planets and beyond, through all systems and between them.

5. Ask to heal all connections and interactions with the fourteen Planetary Grids: the Earth Grid, Mind Grid, Life Grid, Light Grid, Protection Grid, Transformation Grid, Regeneration Grid, Transmutation Grid, Creation Grid, the Well of Life at the Center of the Earth, the Fire of Life at the Center of the Earth, the Interspace Grid, Sustenance Grid, and Compassion Grid. Ask for these healings for Earth and all other planets and between them, all lifetimes and between them, through all dimensions and multidimensions and between them of your multidimensional Be-ing.

6. Ask to cancel forever ALL KARMA AND ALL KARMIC CONTRACTS WITH ALL DAMAGE AND DISCONNECTIONS AND

ALL SOURCES OF THEM, INCLUDING FROM THE SOURCE OF ALL EVIL AND ALL ITS CREATIONS AND MANIFESTATIONS, THROUGH ALL OF THESE SYSTEMS on Earth and all other planets and between them, through all lifetimes and between them, all dimensions and multidimensions and between them, of and between all dimensions of your multidimensional Be-ing.

7. Next, ask to ANNIHILATE, EXTINGUISH, UNCREATE, AND OBLITERATE FROM THESE SYSTEMS FOREVER THE SOURCE OF ALL EVIL AND ALL ITS CREATIONS AND MANIFESTATIONS, including all damage and negative interference of all types, from Earth and all other planets and between them, all lifetimes and between them, through all dimensions and multidimensions and between them, of and between all dimensions of your multidimensional Be-ing.

8. Now ask to SEAL THESE SYSTEMS AND ALL THEIR COMPONENTS, TRANSFORMERS, CONNECTIONS, AND INTERACTIONS FOREVER AGAINST THE SOURCE OF ALL EVIL AND ALL ITS CREATIONS AND MANIFESTATIONS. Ask to SEAL THEM FOR THE LIGHT FOREVER, and UNTO THE LIGHT AND UNTO PROTECTION FOREVER. Ask to cancel all karma and all karmic contracts preventing this total sealing. Ask for these from Earth and all other planets and between them, all lifetimes and between them, all dimensions and multidimensions and between them, of and between all dimensions of your multidimensional Be-ing.

9. Request these healings fully, completely, permanently, and forever, through all the levels and components of your Be-ing, through all dimensions, all connections, all systems and between them, through all multidimensions and between them, of and between all dimensions of your multidimensional Be-ing.

10. Ask for these healings immediately and instantly, past, present, and future, forever and NOW.

11. Thank Divine Director, the Lords of Karma, and the Karmic Board.

Note: Once you have completed Process XVIII, add the following: I request all appropriate Creational, DNA, Mind Grid, and other repatternings and reprogrammings needed for these healings.

Process XVIII   Re-Creation and Replacement

YOUR CREATION IS AN ENERGY COMPONENT, A COMPUTER PROGRAMMING BASED upon and derived from the central programming of the planetary and Galactic Mind Grid and beyond. Where there is significant energy damage, it is often easier for the Lords of Karma and Divine Director to replace a damaged component instead of repairing it or healing it. This is also true of your Creation. Planetary and Galactic (and Universal and Cosmic) damage replicates in the creation of all life. This process is to replace the damaged planetary Mind Grid as it manifests in your individual Creation. The process will result in the closing of your Crown for about a week as the reprogramming and replacements are made. You may feel periods of anxiety during this closing, but you are fully safe. This is the most important process and healing of *Essential Energy Balancing II.*

If you are bringing in a Goddess, it is important to make the requests of this process for you, your Goddess, your union, total union, and ascension.

1. Ask Divine Director, the Lords of Karma, and the Karmic Board to REPLACE AND RE-CREATE THE PROGRAMMING OF YOUR CREATION, deleting from it all attacks, damage, access, negative programming, and negative interference of all types by the Source of All Evil and all its creations and manifestations. Ask to delete, also, all dis-ease, all that prevents your evolution and ascension, all that obstructs or prevents the full opening and function of your energy, all that obstructs or prevents the full manifestation of your life purpose, all that keeps you from manifesting your full connection with the Light, and all that prevents the manifesting of your full Light and life force. (You may add to this list.)

2. Request to REPLACE ALL COMPONENTS AND CONNECTIONS THROUGH ALL SYSTEMS THAT MANIFEST CREATIONAL DAMAGE OR EVIL, AND RECONNECT ALL SYSTEMS TO THE PURITY AND PERFECTION OF THE LIGHT.

3. Ask that the Source of All Evil, all its creations and manifestations, and the negatives above be ANNIHILATED, EXTINGUISHED, UNCREATED, AND OBLITERATED from your new Creation and energy through all systems.

4. Ask that your new Creation be programmed to CANCEL ALL KARMA AND ALL KARMIC CONTRACTS with the above deletions, with the Source of All Evil and all of its creations and manifestations.

5. Request to HEAL AND REGENERATE ALL DAMAGE to your Creation and all systems, replacing all components and connections that are too damaged to easily heal, in full accordance with the Light. Ask for full reconnection of all energies, and for full and optimal function of all components, connections, and systems. Ask for total safety and protection for your new Creation and all components, connections, and systems forever.

6. Ask to SEAL YOUR NEW CREATION AGAINST ALL THE ABOVE DELETIONS AND THE SOURCE OF ALL EVIL AND ALL OF ITS CREATIONS AND MANIFESTATIONS FOREVER. Ask to SEAL YOUR NEW CREATION FOR THE LIGHT FOREVER, and UNTO THE LIGHT AND UNTO PROTECTION FOREVER. Ask to cancel all karma and all karmic contracts that prevent this total sealing.

7. Request all of these things in the name of the Light: from Earth and all other planets and between them, all lifetimes and between them, all dimensions and between them, through all multidimensions and between them, of and between all dimensions of your multidimensional Be-ing.

8. Ask for these things fully, completely, permanently, and forever, through all the levels and components of your Be-ing, through all dimensions, all connections, all systems and between them,

through all multidimensions and between them of your multi-dimensional Be-ing.

9. Ask for these healings immediately and instantly under Karmic Law, past, present, and future, forever and NOW.

10. Thank Divine Director, the Lords of Karma, and the Karmic Board.

Universal Healings

a) Repeat the process above for your I-AM Presence.

b) Repeat the process above for all planetary creation, all Creation on all levels, and for all Be-ings, all life and all the Light.

If you are bringing in a Goddess: You have already made these requests for you, your Goddess, your union, total union, and ascension. To this add the following:

a) Do the full process above to REPLACE AND RE-CREATE THE PROGRAMMING OF THE CREATION OF YOUR UNION.

Process XIX   Vibrational Sealing

THERE IS A LIMIT BEYOND WHICH THE SOURCE OF ALL EVIL, OR ANY EVIL, cannot reach to harm you. This process is to raise your energy beyond that limit by means of the full activation of your positive DNA. For Galactic Karma, you will need at least twenty-four strands reconnected and activated to achieve this, but the total possible number of strands is actually eighty-one. By asking for the full complement, you will be given the optimal number for your individual evolution and needs.

As always, remember to make the request for you, your Goddess, your union, total union, and ascension, if you are bringing in a Goddess.

1. Ask Divine Director, the Lords of Karma, and the Karmic Board to RAISE YOUR TOTAL ENERGY VIBRATION above and beyond the level where the Source of All Evil, or any evil, in all its creations and manifestations can affect, attack, or harm you in any way.

2. Next ask to CLEAR, HEAL, RECONNECT, AND FULLY ACTIVATE THE FULL COMPLEMENT OF DNA THAT IS APPROPRIATE FOR YOU.

3. Request that your fully healed, reconnected, and activated DNA, and your fully raised energy vibration be returned to complete perfection and SEALED FOREVER AGAINST THE SOURCE OF ALL EVIL AND ALL OF ITS MANIFESTATIONS AND CREATIONS, FOR THE LIGHT FOREVER and UNTO THE LIGHT AND UNTO PROTECTION FOREVER.

4. Ask to receive ALL CREATIONAL, DNA, MIND GRID, AND OTHER REPATTERNINGS AND REPROGRAMMINGS that are needed for this healing.

5. Ask for these healings on Earth and all other planets and between them, through all lifetimes and between them, through all

dimensions and multidimensions and between them, of and between all dimensions of your multidimensional Be-ing.

6. Ask for these healings:

> Fully, completely, permanently, and forever,
>
> Through all the levels and components of your Being, all dimensions, all connections, all systems and between them, all lifetimes and between them, through all dimensions and multidimensions and between them, of and between all dimensions of your multidimensional Be-ing.
>
> Immediately and instantly,
>
> Past, present, future,
>
> NOW.

7. Thank Divine Director, the Lords of Karma, and the Karmic Board.

Universal Healing

a) Repeat the above process for the Earth and all planets, our Solar System and all solar systems, our Galaxy and all galaxies, our Universe and all universes, our Cosmos and all cosmos—and beyond, and for all Be-ings, all life, and all the Light.

Process XX   The Radiance of the Goddess

AS STRANGE AS IT SEEMS, THE GODDESSES (AND OTHER LIGHT BE-INGS—ANGELS, archangels, Ascended Masters, the Lords of Karma, and Karmic Boards) are vulnerable to damage and harm, as they are part of Creation that was damaged by the Source of All Evil. Stranger yet is the idea that people in bodies on Earth are needed to heal that damage for Be-ings of far higher Light than we can even imagine. Yet it is so, and this process is a request to heal the Goddesses and all of the Light, who in turn are the sources of healing for all people and all life.

If you are bringing in a Goddess, be sure to make these requests for you, your Goddess, your union, total union, and ascension.

1. Ask Divine Director, the Lords of Karma, and the Karmic Board to MAKE THE GODDESS ENERGY ON AND FOR EARTH, AND ALL GODDESSES AND BE-INGS OF THE LIGHT ON EARTH AND ALL OTHER PLANETS, SO STRONG AND SO WHOLE THAT THEY ARE TOTALLY INVULNERABLE to the Source of All Evil and all its creations and manifestations forever.

2. Request the TOTAL HEALING AND REGENERATION of all Goddesses and all Goddess energy and Light Be-ings, on Earth and all other planets and between them, through all lifetimes and between them, through all dimensions and multidimensions and between them, of and between all dimensions of their multidimensional Be-ings. Ask to replace with absolute purity of the Light all components, connections, and systems that are too damaged to readily heal, and all that carry the replication of damage or evil. Request the reconnection of all energies, and that all components, connections, and systems be brought to full and optimal purification, activation, and function, in absolute safety and protection forever in accordance with the Light.

3. Ask that all Goddesses, Goddess energy, and Light Be-ings be SEALED AGAINST THE SOURCE OF ALL EVIL AND ALL ITS CREATIONS AND MANIFESTATIONS FOREVER, BE SEALED FOR THE LIGHT FOREVER, and BE SEALED UNTO THE LIGHT AND UNTO PROTECTION FOREVER.

4. Request these healings:

   Fully, completely, permanently, and forever,

   Through all the levels and components of all Goddesses, Goddess energy and Light Be-ings, through all dimensions, all connections, all systems and between them, through all multidimensions and between them, of and between all dimensions of their multidimensional Be-ings.

   Immediately and instantly,

   Past, present, and future,

   NOW.

5. Thank Divine Director, the Lords of Karma, and the Karmic Board.

Universal Healing

   a) Do the above process for your own Goddess, whether or not you are bringing Her into your energy.

Process XXI   Sealing the Planet

PLANETS HAVE KARMA TOO, AND ALL BE-INGS CREATED PARTAKE IN THE KARMA OF the planet they work for or are incarnated upon. Earth has carried karma with the Source of All Evil from its beginning. Alien conquest from the Galaxy and beyond has been the source of most of the wrong and the suffering of Earth's people. It is time to end that karma forever—for the good of all—and return the Earth and all Be-ings to the Light.

If you are bringing in a Goddess, this process is for you, your Goddess, your union, total union, and ascension, as well as for the Earth.

1. Ask to speak with the Lords of Karma, Divine Director, and the Karmic Board, as well as Nada, Light Mother, St. Germaine, and all the protecting angels and archangels of the Earth and Solar System.

2. Request to CANCEL AND END FOREVER THE EARTH'S AND ALL EARTH BE-INGS' KARMA AND KARMIC CONTRACTS WITH THE SOURCE OF ALL EVIL AND ALL ITS CREATIONS AND MANIFESTATIONS. Ask to cancel forever for Earth and all Earth Be-ings all planetary, Solar System, and Galactic Karma with all attacks, evil vows and curses, intergalactic warfare and weaponry, conquest by evil forces, damage and harm by evil of all types, access by evil, negative interference, negative programming and mechanisms, prevention and blockage of planetary evolution and ascension, obstruction and blockage of the evolution and ascension of all Be-ings, and prevention of Goddess energy and the Light on Earth and all planets.

3. Next, ask that the Source of All Evil and all the negatives listed above be ANNIHILATED, EXTINGUISHED, UNCREATED, AND OBLITERATED FROM THE SOLAR SYSTEM AND GALAXY, AND THE EARTH AND ALL EARTH BE-INGS, INCLUDING ALL LIGHT BE-INGS, IMMEDIATELY, INSTANTLY, AND FOREVER.

4. Request FOR THE PLANET, SOLAR SYSTEM, AND GALAXY, AND ALL BE-INGS TOTAL HEALING AND REGENERATION OF ALL DAMAGE, replacing any components, connections, and systems that are too damaged to easily heal or that are carrying evil, negative programming or mechanisms. Ask for full reconnection of all energies, and for full and optimal function and perfection of all components, connections, systems, and Be-ings in accordance with the Light. Ask for total safety and protection for all of the above from the Source of All Evil, and all evil, forever.

5. Ask to SEAL THE GALAXY, SOLAR SYSTEM, EARTH, AND ALL BE-INGS, INCLUDING ALL LIGHT BE-INGS, AGAINST THE SOURCE OF ALL EVIL AND ALL ITS CREATIONS AND MANIFESTATIONS FOREVER. Request to SEAL THE GALAXY, SOLAR SYSTEM, EARTH, AND ALL BE-INGS FOR THE LIGHT FOREVER, and UNTO THE LIGHT AND UNTO PROTECTION FOREVER. Ask to cancel all karma and all karmic contracts that prevent this total sealing.

6. Request ALL APPROPRIATE REPATTERNINGS AND REPROGRAMMINGS—CREATIONAL, DNA, MIND GRID, AND ALL OTHERS—that are needed for these healings.

7. Ask for these things in the name of the Light, on Earth and all other planets and between them, through all lifetimes and between them, through all dimensions and multidimensions and between them, of and between all dimensions of the Galaxy, Solar System, and Earth's multidimensional Be-ing, all Be-ings, all life, and all the Light.

8. Ask for these things fully, completely, permanently, and forever, through all the levels and components of Earth's and all Be-ings, all dimensions, all connections, all systems and between them, through all multidimensions and between them, of and between all dimensions of the Galaxy, Solar System, and Earth's multidimensional Be-ing, all Be-ings, all life, and all the Light.

9. Request these healings from above the Pure Light beyond Galactic Creation to below the Well of Life and Fire of Life at the Center of the Earth and all planets and beyond, and between of all of these, through all multidimensions and between them, of and between all dimensions of Earth's multidimensional Be-ing, all Be-ings, all life, and all the Light.

10. Ask for these healings immediately and instantly under Karmic Law, past, present, and future, forever and NOW.

11. Thank Divine Director, the Lords of Karma, the Karmic Board, Nada, Light Mother, St. Germaine, and all the angels and archangels.

12. Know that it is done.

Universal Healings Repeat the process above for each of the following:

    a) The Light, and all Sources and Be-ings of the Light

    b) All the Goddesses, Goddess unions, total unions, and ascensions

    c) Earth's ascension, and the ascension of all Earth Be-ings

    d) The ascension of our Galaxy and all galaxies, our Solar System, and all solar systems

Process XXII   Final Sealing and Shielding

THE FIRST PART OF THIS PROCESS ASKS FOR THE TOTAL SEALING OF THE EARTH, Solar System, and Galaxy against the Source of All Evil and all evil. The second part asks Archangel Michael for the total defense, shielding, and regeneration of the Earth, Solar System, and all planetary life, including your own life. The final request is to awaken all Light Be-ings and free them to defend and heal the Earth and all Be-ings. If you are bringing in a Goddess, you will find appropriate instructions for you at the end of the process.

Part I

1. Ask to speak with the Lords of Karma, Divine Director, the Karmic Board, Nada, St. Germaine, Archangel Michael, and all the protecting angels and archangels of the Earth, Solar System, and Galaxy.

2. Request to SEAL THE LIST BELOW FOREVER AGAINST THE SOURCE OF ALL EVIL AND ALL ITS CREATIONS AND MANI-FESTATIONS, all attacks, all evil vows and curses; all intergalactic, interplanetary, and intraplanetary warfare; all conquest by evil forces, all damage and harm by evil of all types, all access by evil, all negative interference, all negative programming and mechanisms, all prevention and blockage of planetary evolution and ascension, all obstruction and blockage of the evolution and ascension of all Be-ings, and all prevention of the Goddess energy and the Light on Earth and all planets. Request this sealing for:

   The Galaxy
   The Solar System
   All planets of the Solar System and Galaxy
   The Earth
   All Solar System and Galactic grids and structures

All grids for all planets of the Solar System and Galaxy

All Earth Planetary Grids

The Earth Grid

The Well Life at the Center of the Earth and all planets

The Fire of Life at the Center of Earth and all planets

All continents and land masses on Earth and all planets

All bodies of water on Earth and all planets

All Be-ings, all life, and all the Light

Ask to SEAL THE LIST ABOVE FOR THE LIGHT FOREVER, and UNTO THE LIGHT AND UNTO PROTECTION FOREVER.

3. Request the CANCELLATION OF ALL KARMA AND ALL KARMIC CONTRACTS for the list above with the Source of All Evil, all its creations and manifestations, and all the negatives and evils listed above. Ask that any karma or karmic contracts preventing the full sealing of the Earth, Solar System, and Galaxy be canceled and ended immediately and forever NOW.

4. Ask to ANNIHILATE, EXTINGUISH, UNCREATE, OBLITERATE, AND TRANSMUTE FOR THE LIGHT all evil and residue of evil from the Earth, Solar System, and Galaxy as listed above.

5. Request for the Galaxy, Solar System, and Earth as above TOTAL HEALING AND REGENERATION OF ALL DAMAGE, replacing all components, connections, and systems that are too damaged to easily heal or that have been destroyed, or that are carrying negative or evil programming or mechanisms. Ask for full reconnection of all energies, and for full and optimal function and perfection of all components, connections, grids, systems, and Be-ings in accordance with the Light. Request the total safety and protection for the full list above forever.

IF YOU ARE BRINGING IN A GODDESS: Make the requests above for you, your Goddess, your union, total union, and your ascension. This is all one process and request. Do the full process, and then the processes below.

Part II

1. Now, ask Archangel Michael, Divine Director, the Lords of Karma, the Karmic Board, St. Germaine, and Nada to install ARCHANGEL MICHAEL'S SWORD of Truth and Protection in each of the following. If there is a "no" to any of these requests, you will be told; ask what to do. Ask where the Sword is to be installed in each item on the list, and request that it be installed and activated immediately, permanently, continuously, and forever.

   The Solar System
   All planets of the Solar System
   The Earth
   All Solar System grids and structures
   All grids for all planets of the Solar System
   All Earth Planetary Grids
   The Earth Grid
   The Well of Life at the Center of the Earth and all planets
   The Fire of Life at the Center of the Earth and all planets
   All continents and land masses on Earth and all planets
   All bodies of water on Earth and all planets
   All Be-ings, all life, and all the Light

2. Repeat the process above asking for ARCHANGEL MICHAEL'S KARMIC SHIELD for each of the items. Ask where the Shield is to be installed in each, and request that it be done and activated immediately, permanently, continuously, and forever for each item on the list above.

3. Next, ask to install ARCHANGEL MICHAEL'S CHALICE of Healing and Regeneration in each of the items above. Ask where the Chalice is to be installed in each, and request that it be done and activated immediately, permanently, continuously, and forever for each of the items in the list.

4. Ask for FULL MERGING, FUSION, AND SEALING as appropriate for all of the Swords, Shields, and Chalices above, and ask

again for full activation, immediately, permanently, continuously, and forever. Ask that the activation be fully protected.

5. Request the ability to use Archangel Michael's Sword effectively and decisively when it is needed to fight evil and protect the Light. Ask to know when fighting is appropriate and for Archangel Michael's presence, protection, and guidance when you do it. Pick up the Sword. It is time to expel the Source of All Evil, and all evil, from the Earth and all planets forever.

IF YOU ARE BRINGING IN A GODDESS: Ask for the Sword, Shield, and Chalice for you, your Goddess, your union, total union, and ascension. Do this all in one request. Ask where each is to be placed, and request placement, installation, and activation. Ask that the Swords, Shields, and Chalices be merged, fused, and sealed as appropriate. Request full activation immediately, permanently, continuously, and forever. Give your Goddess the ability to use the Sword safely as needed.

Note: After twenty-four hours, check to see if each Sword, Shield, and Chalice has been fully installed and activated. You may need to repeat parts of these requests. If something continues to be inactivated after the second request, ask Divine Director and Archangel Michael what is needed.

Part III

1. Ask for the FULL AWAKENING AND REACTIVATION OF ALL LIGHT BE-INGS on Earth and all planets through all multi-dimensions and between them, immediately, permanently, and forever. Ask that all Be-ings of the Light be sealed forever against the Source of All Evil and all its creations and manifestations, for the Light forever, and unto the Light and unto protection forever.

2. If you are shown particular Be-ings awakening, ASK THEIR HELP in protecting, defending, and healing the Earth and all Be-ings.

3. Ask for YOUR OWN FULL AWAKENING AND REACTIVATION IN SERVICE TO THE PLANET AND ALL PLANETS immediately,

permanently, and forever. Ask that you be sealed forever against the Source of All Evil and all its creations and manifestations, sealed for the Light forever, and unto the Light and unto protection forever.

IF YOU ARE BRINGING IN A GODDESS: Ask for the completion, awakening, and full activation of you, your Goddess, your union, total union, and ascension—immediately, permanently, and forever. Ask that you be sealed forever against the Source of All Evil and all its creations and manifestations, for the Light forever, and unto the Light and unto protection forever.

Completion

1. Request all APPROPRIATE REPATTERNINGS AND REPRO-GRAMMINGS FOR THESE HEALINGS: CREATIONAL, DNA, MIND GRID, AND ALL OTHERS.

2. Ask for all of these healings in the name of the Light, on Earth and all other planets and between them, through all lifetimes and between them, through all dimensions, multidimensions and between them, of and between all dimensions of you, the Earth, the Solar System, the Galaxy, and all planets' multidimensional Be-ings, for all Be-ings, all life, and all the Light.

   IF YOU ARE BRINGING IN A GODDESS, ADD: and for you, your Goddess, your union, total union, and ascension.

3. Ask for these things fully, completely, permanently, and forever, through all the levels and components of all Be-ings, all dimensions, all connections, all systems and between them, through all dimensions and multidimensions and between them, of and between all dimensions of all multidimensional Be-ings.

   IF YOU ARE BRINGING IN A GODDESS, ADD: and for you, your Goddess, your union, total union, and ascension, among and amid all Great Goddess unions. And for the Great Goddess and all Goddesses to walk the Earth and all planets in full manifestation, with and through their chosen women, in peace and safety forever.

4. Request these healings immediately and instantly under Karmic Law, past, present, and future, forever and NOW.

5. Thank the Lords of Karma, Divine Director, the Karmic Board, Nada, St. Germaine, Archangel Michael, and all the protecting angels and archangels of the Earth, Solar System, and Galaxy.

6. Know that it is done.

Process XXIII   Final Banishing

THE SOURCE OF ALL EVIL IS THE CONQUEST OF THE LIGHT BY BE-INGS FROM other worlds who seek to destroy all life and evolution and to take over the Cosmos. As these Be-ings affect our Galaxy, they primarily include the negative Greys (the stereotyped big-eyed ET character) and Orion (who appear as lizards). The signature of the negative Greys is the many abduction experiences by people from all over the world. The signature of Orion is energy implants transmitting images of spiders, snakes, lizards, squid, or other "nasties." A more insidious signature of the negative Greys and others of evil is in mechanisms and "magick spells" or curses transmitting blockages and energy destructions that recur over many lifetimes, remaining in our energy through many reincarnations. Other alien scavengers of greater and lesser danger are present on the planet as well.

Any of these and more can take over and work through humans of greedy, vengeful, or negative intent. They can also operate on their own, and they cause great harm. This process is to end whatever still remains of these Be-ings on Earth, and through our Solar System and Galaxy, and for all life on Earth and all planets.

If you are bringing in a Goddess, make all requests for you, your Goddess, your union, total union, and ascension.

1. Ask to speak with Divine Director, the Lords of Karma, the Karmic Board, and Archangels Michael, Ashtar, and Metatron.

2. Request of them to BANISH FROM ALL OF YOUR ENERGY, AND FROM THE EARTH, SOLAR SYSTEM, GALAXY, AND ALL OF BE-ING, ALL NEGATIVE ALIENS AND ACCESS BY NEGATIVE ALIENS OF ALL TYPES. Request the ending of all negative interference and negative and evil effects, all negative and evil implants, curses and spells, for all Be-ings and planets. Request the full freedom of all life on Earth and all planets to manifest our

individual and planetary, Solar System, and Galactic destinies without negative or evil interference and in peace.

3. Continue with the four part process as follows:

   a) Ask to CANCEL ALL KARMA AND ALL KARMIC CONTRACTS with the above alien energies, access, and interference.

   b) Request to ANNIHILATE, EXTINGUISH, UNCREATE, OBLITERATE, and remove from your energy, and all energy forever, all negative and evil aliens and their energies, access, implants, mechanisms, interference, and all effects and harm.

   c) Request the total HEALING AND REGENERATION of all damage from the above in full accordance with the Light. This includes the replacement of all components, connections, and systems too damaged to easily heal or that have been destroyed, are missing, or are carrying replication of interference or evil.

   Ask that ALL SYSTEMS, COMPONENTS, AND CONNECTIONS BE RETURNED TO THE COMPLETE PURITY AND PERFECTION THAT IS OUR ORIGINAL CREATIONAL BIRTHRIGHT for us and for the Earth, Solar System, and Galaxy, and ask for full reconnection and the return of full and optimal function and opening of all components, connections, and systems. Request total safety and protection now and forever.

   d) Ask to SEAL YOUR ENERGY, AND THE EARTH, SOLAR SYSTEM, AND GALAXY AGAINST ALL OF THE ABOVE EVILS AND THEIR NEGATIVE AND EVIL EFFECTS FOREVER, FOR THE LIGHT FOREVER, and UNTO THE LIGHT AND UNTO PROTECTION FOREVER.

4. Request ALL APPROPRIATE REPATTERNINGS AND REPROGRAMMINGS—CREATIONAL, DNA, MIND GRID, AND ALL OTHERS ON ALL LEVELS—that are needed for these healings.

5. Request these healings in the name of the Light, on Earth and all other planets and between them, through all lifetimes and between them, through all dimensions and multidimensions and between them, of and between all dimensions of all multi-dimensional Be-ings, all Be-ings, all life, and all the Light.

6. Ask for these things, fully, completely, permanently, and forever through all the levels and components of all Be-ings, all dimensions, all connections, all systems and between them, all lifetimes and planets and between them, through all dimensions and multidimensions and between them of all multidimensional Be-ings, all Be-ings, all life, and all the Light.

7. Ask for these healings immediately and instantly under Karmic Law, past, present, and future, forever and NOW.

8. Thank Divine Director, the Lords of Karma, the Karmic Board, Archangels Michael, Ashtar, and Metatron, and all the Be-ings of Light participating in these healings.

9. Know that you are free.

Process XXIV   Planetary Activation

THE FIRST GREAT GODDESS UNION OF TWENTY-ONE GODDESSES ENTERED THE
Earth Grid February 11 through 14, 2000. They have joined with twenty-
one women and returned to Earth through their energy. These women
know who they are. They are only the first of many Goddesses, Goddess
unions, and Great Goddess unions to come to heal this planet, but they are
the first Goddesses to return to us in more than a thousand years.

The process that follows is to activate the Great Goddess unions. It
brings the Goddesses to Earth, anchors them to this planet, then joins and
manifests their Be-ing with the women they have chosen to manifest
through. Though this Planetary Activation was requested on February 23,
2000, and completed three days later, many more Goddesses and Great
Goddess unions (groups of twenty-one Goddesses each) are entering this
planet. Their return means the anchoring of Light upon the Earth and the
total expulsion of all evil. A critical mass of many making the request is
important for the Goddesses' return.

A Goddess union consists of a woman and her Goddess. A Great
Goddess union is twenty-one Goddess unions joined into one Be-ing.

Please note: Only women will bring in Goddesses, men will not.
Women completing *Essential Energy Balancing* and *Essential Energy
Balancing II* will know if a Goddess has chosen them to manifest through.
The Goddesses do the choosing, not the women.

1. Ask to speak with the Lords of Karma, Divine Director, the
    Karmic Board, and Archangels Michael, Ashtar, and Metatron.
    Also ask for the presence and protection of the Guardians of the
    Four Directions, plus the Guardians of Above, Below, and the
    Center of the planet, as well as the guardians and protectors of
    each Goddess. You may cast a Wiccan Circle of protection with
    these Be-ings, if you wish.

2. Ask to BRING THE GODDESSES OF ALL GREAT GODDESS UNIONS INTO ALL THE PLANETARY GRIDS.

3. Request the FULL ANCHORING of the Goddesses of all Great Goddess unions into the Earth and all Planetary Grids. Ask that they PREPARE AND STABILIZE THE GRIDS for the return of the Goddess to Earth.

4. Ask to BRING EACH GODDESS THROUGH THE PLANETARY GRIDS AND INTO THEIR CHOSEN WOMEN.

5. Ask the Goddesses to MERGE AND FUSE FULLY WITH THEIR CHOSEN WOMEN, AND THAT EACH GODDESS UNION BE COMPLETED AND SEALED. Ask that these Goddess unions be MERGED INTO ONE GREAT GODDESS UNION, and the merging fused and sealed. Ask that each Goddess union and all Great Goddess unions be fully SEALED AGAINST ALL EVIL FOREVER, FOR THE LIGHT FOREVER, and UNTO THE LIGHT AND UNTO PROTECTION FOREVER.

6. Request the complete ESTABLISHMENT, CLEARING, AND FULL CONNECTION of all components, systems, cords, channels, and pathways joining each Goddess with her chosen woman. Request the FULL CONNECTION OF ALL THE GODDESS UNIONS WITH EACH OTHER, and all the Great Goddess unions into one.

7. Ask for the FULL OPENING OF ALL CONNECTIONS AND SENSORY PERCEPTIONS of each woman with her Goddess.

8. Request FULL ACTIVATION OF EACH GODDESS UNION, EACH GREAT GODDESS UNION, AND OF ALL THE GREAT GODDESS UNIONS immediately, instantly, and forever.

9. Request all appropriate CREATIONAL REPATTERNINGS, DNA REPATTERNINGS, MIND GRID REPATTERNINGS, AND ALL OTHER REPATTERNINGS AND REPROGRAMMINGS that are needed, including repatternings and reprogrammings for the planet, Solar System, and Galaxy.

10. Ask for these healings in the name of the Light, on Earth and all other planets and between them, through all lifetimes and between them, through all dimensions and multidimensions and between them, of and between all dimensions of all Goddesses, Goddess Be-ings, and Goddess unions, among and amid all Great Goddess unions.

   IF YOU ARE BRINGING IN A GODDESS, ADD: and for you, your Goddess, your union, total union, and ascension.

11. Ask for these things fully, completely, permanently, and forever through all the levels and components of all Goddesses and Goddess Be-ings, all dimensions, all connections, all systems and between them, all lifetimes and planets and between them, through all dimensions, multidimensions and between them, of and between all dimensions of all Goddesses, Goddess Be-ings, and Goddess unions, among and amid all Great Goddess unions, for the Great Goddess and all Goddesses to walk the Earth and all planets in safety, peace, and joy forever.

12. Request these healings immediately and instantly under Karmic Law, past, present, and future, forever and NOW.

13. Thank the Lords of Karma, Divine Director, the Karmic Board, Archangels Michael, Ashtar, and Metatron, the Guardians of the Directions, and all the Be-ings of Light participating in these healings. Thank the Goddesses for coming back to Earth.

14. Rejoice!

To Bring in a Goddess

If you have been chosen to bring your Goddess into your energy for Her to fully manifest through you, you will know by now. Your Goddess Herself will tell you, or Divine Director or the Karmic Board will make the information evident. Only women will bring in their Goddesses, though everyone has a Goddess and may be in contact with Her. Those women who are chosen by their Goddesses have been selected for a variety of reasons. They are women on an ascension path, willing to do the work of clearing their karma, and of a Light level high enough to support Goddess energy merged with their own. Most are seriously doing some form of planetary service or service to people or animals; they may be healers, teachers, caretakers of animals or land, activists, or otherwise good role models for others and making a difference. They are women willing to devote their lives to the Goddess and their own Goddess, as well as to a path of service.

This is not a job for everyone, and while those suited for it will enjoy it tremendously, those not suited for it may find it more than they wish to complicate their lives with. Bringing in a Goddess will totally change your life, from under your skin to without. First of all, you will never be alone again, and you will never be unguided. Your choices and free will on many occasions will come second to your Goddess's needs. You also may find that your Goddess needs a great deal of healing, and She has probably been under a great deal of attack. It will be up to you, with Divine Director, the Karmic Board and these processes, to heal Her and to end those attacks upon both of you. You will learn what She needs and make the requests for Her. When She is merged with you, Her healing needs become your own, and if She is being attacked, you are being attacked with Her.

The processes for clearing your karma and of the subsequent closing of your Crown for repatterning are not always easy or pleasant, and they are extended in those bringing in a Goddess. You must clear much more of your karma on all levels when bringing in a Goddess than you would need to for ascension without. You will also need to complete *Essential Energy Balancing III* when it is published and the release of your karma through the Universe and Cosmos. All of this requires extended, dedicated, and often unpleasant work on your part, but if your Goddess chooses you and you complete the work, you will find it worth your while.

If you still wish to go further, and you have been invited by your Goddess to bring Her in, the following is a summary of what is needed. Permission is required of the Lords of Karma, the Karmic Board, Divine Director, and your Goddess to do this. With that given, the following processes must be done, using the exact wording given below. If you receive a "no" to any request, ask what is needed to release the "no" and follow instructions, or ask to cancel all karma and all karmic contracts from Earth and all other planets, all lifetimes and between them, that may be the source of the "no."

1. You must first complete all of the processes in my book *Essential Energy Balancing*. You must be working on the clearing of your Earth karma, or have completed it, and have the ability to make requests of the Lords of Karma. Your Energy Selves must be fully fused into your energy and your Light Body activated. If you have not already done these things, get the book and do them now. You may be told at some point that you need to repeat some of the processes. If you are, do so.

2. Make the request of Divine Director, the Lords of Karma, and the Karmic Board to clear, heal, reconnect, and fully activate the full

complement of your DNA, if you haven't done so already. Only a "yes" is needed here, no process is required. You only need to do this once.

3. Request formally of Divine Director, the Lords of Karma, and the Karmic Board that you bring in your Goddess to fully merge with you and live with you on Earth. Ask for the name of the Goddess you will bring in. She is usually the Goddess who was named as your Goddess in *Essential Energy Balancing*, but not always. Ask to cancel all karma and all karmic contracts from Earth and all other planets, from all lifetimes and between them, preventing you from bringing your Goddess in. (No process is required, only a "yes.")

4. Ask Divine Director, the Lords of Karma, and the Karmic Board to fully develop, establish, activate, and open all Galactic Cord and Chain of Light components, systems, and connections for you, your Goddess, your union, total union, and ascension. Use Process XI, the Short Process, with the exact wording as follows. Use this process for all other karmic requests as well; it is summarized again below.

    a) Ask to speak with the Lords of Karma and Divine Director.

    b) Make the request for you, your Goddess, your union, total union, and ascension, on Earth, all other planets and between them, through all lifetimes and between them, through all dimensions and multidimensions and between them, of and between all dimensions of your multidimensional Be-ing.

    c) Ask for these things fully, completely, permanently, and forever, through all the levels and components of your Be-ing, all dimensions, all connections, all systems, and between them, through all multidimensions and between them of and between all dimensions of you, your Goddess, your union's, total union's, and ascension's multidimensional Be-ing.

d) Ask for these things immediately and instantly, past, present, and future, forever and NOW.

e) Thank the Divine Director, the Lords of Karma, the Karmic Board, and your Goddess.

5. Request the full and complete healing of your Goddess, in accordance with the Light. Ask to cancel all karma and all karmic contracts from all planets, lifetimes, and between them, through all dimensions, multidimensions and between them, that could prevent Her total healing. (No process is required here, only a "yes." Use the above precise wording. If you are shown what needs healing, use the Short Process to request that it be done.)

6. Ask to cancel ALL karma and ALL karmic contracts in totality from all lifetimes and incarnations on all planets and between them, including for this lifetime, for you, your Goddess, your union, total union, and ascension, past, present, future, forever, and NOW. (No process is needed here, only a "yes.")

7. Do Process XVIII: Re-Creation and Replacement in this book.

8. Do the two processes given below from *Essential Energy Balancing III*. These are the Sword, Chalice, Shield Fusion, and Interdimensional Sword, Chalice, and Shield. They offer more complete protection for you and for your Goddess than you have received until now.

Sword, Chalice, Shield Fusion

In Process III of this book (and in *Reliance on the Light*), you were given the Sword, Chalice, and Shield of Archangel Michael. This time these articles of protection are to be installed in your Creational programming—for you, your Goddess, your union, your total union, your ascension, and in your Galactic Cord system as well. The fusion, sealing, and activation of these articles is the fusion, sealing, and activation of your Goddess union. As a number of protecting archangels are now present for ascension women and their unions, I am replacing Archangel Michael's name with that of "your

Dimensional Archangel" in the process. Your Dimensional Archangel may be Archangel Michael or another Archangel of the Light.

1. Ask to speak with the Lords of Karma, Divine Director, your Dimensional Archangel, and the Karmic Board. Request the REPROGRAMMING OF YOUR CREATION TO INSTALL YOUR DIMENSIONAL ARCHANGEL'S SWORD OF PROTECTION AND TRUTH IN YOUR ENERGY, YOUR GODDESS'S ENERGY, IN THE ENERGY OF YOUR UNION WITH HER, IN YOUR TOTAL UNION, YOUR ASCENSION, AND IN ALL GALACTIC CORD SYSTEMS IN THEIR COMPLETELY SYNCHRONIZED AND COMPLEMENTARY STATE. The Sword is used to fight evil and protect the Light. If at this step or any other of the process, your request is denied, ask what you must do to have it, and follow the directions that will be given to you. Otherwise continue.

2. When the request is granted, ask where the Sword is to be installed in each. There will be six Swords, one in you, one in your Goddess, one in your union, one in your total union, one in your ascension, and one in your Galactic Cord system. They will be in six different places. If the request is granted, but you are not shown locations, you may still continue.

3. Ask that the reprogramming be completed and the Swords be installed.

4. Now REQUEST THE REPROGRAMMING OF YOUR CREATION TO INSTALL YOUR DIMENSIONAL ARCHANGEL'S KARMIC SHIELD IN YOUR ENERGY, YOUR GODDESS'S ENERGY, IN THE ENERGY OF YOUR UNION WITH HER, IN YOUR TOTAL UNION, YOUR ASCENSION, AND IN ALL GALACTIC CORD SYSTEMS IN THEIR COMPLETELY SYNCHRONIZED AND COMPLEMENTARY STATE. The Shield protects you from the return of old karma.

5. If the request is granted, ask where the Shield is to be installed in each. There will be six Shields, one in you, one in your Goddess,

one in your union, one in your total union, one in your ascension, and one in your Galactic Cord system. They will be in six different places. If the request is granted, but you are not shown locations, you may still continue.

6. Ask that the reprogramming be completed and the Shields be installed.

7. Next, REQUEST THE REPROGRAMMING OF YOUR CREATION TO INSTALL YOUR DIMENSIONAL ARCHANGEL'S CHALICE OF HEALING AND REGENERATION IN YOUR ENERGY, YOUR GODDESS'S ENERGY, IN THE ENERGY OF YOUR UNION, IN YOUR TOTAL UNION, YOUR ASCENSION, AND IN ALL GALACTIC CORD SYSTEMS IN THEIR COMPLETELY SYN-CHRONIZED AND COMPLEMENTARY STATE. The Chalice's use is for the automatic self-healing of your energy.

8. If the request is granted, ask where the Chalice is to be installed in each. There will be six Chalices, one in you, one in your Goddess, one in your union, one in your total union, one in your ascension, and one in your Galactic Cord system. They will be in six different places. If the request is granted, but you are not shown locations, continue.

9. Ask that the reprogramming be completed and the Chalices be installed.

10. Now ask for THE FULL REPROGRAMMING OF YOUR CRE-ATION FOR THE FULL, CONTINUOUS, AND PERMANENT ACTIVATION OF THE SWORDS, SHIELDS, AND CHALICES IN YOUR ENERGY, YOUR GODDESS'S ENERGY, IN THE ENERGY OF YOUR UNION, TOTAL UNION, AND ASCENSION, AND IN ALL GALACTIC CORD SYSTEMS FOREVER. Request the com-plete insulation of your energy to protect the full activations. Wait for this to be done; unless you receive a "no" response, it's hap-pening. Ask when to go on.

11. Request the full activation of the Swords, Shields, and Chalices.

12. When all six Swords, Shields, and Chalices in you, your Goddess, your union, total union, ascension, and Galactic Cord systems are fully activated, request the following. Ask the Lords of Karma, Divine Director, the Karmic Board, and your Dimensional Archangel for THE FULL REPROGRAMMING OF YOUR CRE-ATION TO MERGE AND FUSE, AND TO SEAL THE MERGING AND FUSION OF THE SWORDS, CHALICES, AND SHIELDS. The six Swords will be fused together, the six Shields will be fused together, and the six Chalices will be fused together, thereby fus-ing you, your Goddess and your union, total union, and ascen-sion into one. Ask when the fusion and sealing are complete; wait for this before going on.

13. Ask the Lords of Karma, Divine Director, the Karmic Board, and your Dimensional Archangel for THE FULL REPROGRAMMING OF YOUR CREATION TO FULLY ACTIVATE THE FUSION AND SEALING OF THE SWORDS, SHIELDS, AND CHALICES, AND THEREBY FULLY ACTIVATE AND SEAL YOUR UNION WITH YOUR GODDESS.

14. To finish, ask for these healings and reprogrammings in the name of the Light, on Earth and all other planets and between them, through all lifetimes and between them, through all dimensions, multidimensions and between them, of and between all dimen-sions of you and your Goddess's multidimensional Be-ing, union, total union, and ascension.

15. Ask for these things fully, completely, permanently, and forever, through all the levels and components of your Be-ing, all dimensions, all connections, all systems and between them, through all multidimensions and between them of you, your Goddess, your union, total union, and ascension's multi-dimensional Be-ing.

16. Request these healings and reprogrammings immediately and instantly, past, present, and future, forever and NOW.

17. Thank the Lords of Karma, Divine Director, the Karmic Board, and your Dimensional Archangel.

Universal Healings

a) Repeat the full process above, requesting it for ALL CREATION AND ALL ENERGY.

b) Do the full process above, wording it for the CREATION AND ENERGY OF YOUR GODDESS, AND OF YOUR GODDESS UNION.

c) Do the full process above, wording it for THE CREATION AND ENERGY OF ALL THE GODDESSES, GODDESS UNIONS, GREAT GODDESS UNIONS, AND ALL BE-INGS OF THE LIGHT.

d) Repeat the process again, wording it for THE CREATION AND ENERGY OF THE EARTH AND ALL PLANETS, ALL BE-INGS, AND ALL LIFE.

e) Repeat the process above, requesting THE REPROGRAM-MING OF YOUR CREATION AND ENERGY TO INSTALL YOUR DIMENSIONAL ARCHANGEL'S SWORD, SHIELD, AND CHALICE IN YOUR HOME, GARDEN, PETS, CHIL-DREN, AND CAR. (Adults living in the home must make the requests for themselves.) Make sure the articles of protection are all installed and are fully and forever activated.

Interdimensional Sword, Chalice, and Shield

Your Interdimensional Archangel's Sword, Chalice, and Shield protect you through the Solar System's Interspace Grid, the spaces between the dimensions, whereas those of your Dimensional Archangel protect the dimensions only. Added to your Dimensional Archangel's Sword, Chalice, and Shield, those of your Interdimensional Archangel complete the total protections needed for the safety of your Goddess on Earth. Archangel

Ashtar is the keeper of the Earth and Solar System's Interspace Grid, but he is no longer the only Interdimensional protector for Goddess unions. You may be given a different name for your Interdimensional Archangel.

You will note that as in the previous process there are six Swords and Chalices. Here, however, there are seven (instead of six) Shields. The additional Shield, the fusion of the combined protections, is provided by Archangel Metatron. It extends the protection and healing to and through the dimensions and interdimensions of our Galaxy.

1. Ask to speak with the Lords of Karma, Divine Director, your Dimensional Archangel, your Interdimensional Archangel, Metatron, and the Karmic Board. Request the REPROGRAMMING OF YOUR CREATION TO INSTALL YOUR INTERDIMENSIONAL ARCHANGEL'S SWORD OF PROTECTION AND TRUTH IN YOUR ENERGY, YOUR GODDESS'S ENERGY, IN THE ENERGY OF YOUR UNION, IN YOUR TOTAL UNION AND ASCENSION, AND IN ALL GALACTIC CORD SYSTEMS IN THEIR COMPLETELY SYNCHRONIZED AND COMPLEMENTARY STATE. The Sword is used to fight evil between the dimensions. If at this step or any other of the process, your request is denied, ask what you must do to have it and follow the directions that will be given to you. Otherwise continue.

2. If the request is granted, ask where the Sword is to be installed in each. There will be six Swords, one in you, one in your Goddess, one in your union, one in your total union, one in your ascension, and one in your Galactic Cord system. They will be in six different places. If the request is granted, but you are not shown locations, continue.

3. Ask that the reprogramming be completed and the Swords be installed.

4. Now REQUEST THE REPROGRAMMING OF YOUR CREATION TO INSTALL YOUR INTERDIMENSIONAL ARCHANGEL'S KARMIC SHIELD IN YOUR ENERGY, YOUR GODDESS'S

ENERGY, IN THE ENERGY OF YOUR UNION, IN YOUR TOTAL UNION AND ASCENSION, AND IN ALL GALACTIC CORD SYSTEMS IN THEIR COMPLETELY SYNCHRONIZED AND COMPLEMENTARY STATE. There is one further shield— that of Archangel Metatron's fusion of your combined Dimensional and Interdimensional protections—to make a total of seven levels. The Shield protects you from the return of old interplanetary karma.

5. If the request is granted, ask where the Shield is to be installed in each. There will be six Shields, one in you, one in your Goddess, one in your union, one in your total union, one in your ascension, and one in your Galactic Cord system. If you see the seventh, it will be surrounding all the others at the end of this process. The six will be in six different places. If the request is granted, but you are not shown locations, continue.

6. Ask that the reprogramming be completed and the Shields be installed.

7. Next, REQUEST THE REPROGRAMMING OF YOUR CREATION TO INSTALL YOUR INTERDIMENSIONAL ARCHANGEL'S CHALICE OF HEALING AND REGENERATION IN YOUR ENERGY, YOUR GODDESS'S ENERGY, IN THE ENERGY OF YOUR UNION, IN YOUR TOTAL UNION AND ASCENSION, AND IN ALL GALACTIC CORD SYSTEMS IN THEIR COM-PLETELY SYNCHRONIZED AND COMPLEMENTARY STATE. The Chalice's use is for automatic self-healing in the spaces between dimensions.

8. If the request is granted, ask where the Chalice is to be installed in each. There will be six Chalices, one in you, one in your Goddess, one in your union, one in your total union, one in your ascension, and one in your Galactic Cord system. They will be in six different places. If the request is granted, but you are not shown locations, continue.

9. Ask that the reprogramming be completed and the Chalices be installed.

10. Now ask for THE FULL REPROGRAMMING OF YOUR CRE-ATION FOR THE FULL, CONTINUOUS, AND PERMANENT ACTIVATION OF THE SWORDS, SHIELDS, AND CHALICES IN YOUR ENERGY, YOUR GODDESS'S ENERGY, IN THE ENERGY OF YOUR UNION, TOTAL UNION, AND ASCENSION, AND IN ALL GALACTIC CORD SYSTEMS FOREVER. Request the complete insulation of your energy to protect the full activations. Wait for this to be done; unless you receive a "no" response, it's happening. Ask when to go on.

11. Request the full activation of your Interdimensional Archangel's Swords, Shields, and Chalices.

12. When all six Swords, seven Shields, and six Chalices in you, your Goddess, your union, total union and ascension, and all Galactic Cord systems are fully activated, request the following. Ask the Lords of Karma, Divine Director, the Karmic Board, your Dimensional and Interdimensional Archangels, and Archangel Metatron for THE FULL REPROGRAMMING OF YOUR CRE-ATION TO MERGE AND FUSE, AND TO SEAL THE MERGING AND FUSION OF THE SWORDS, SHIELDS, AND CHALICES. The six Swords will be fused together, the seven Shields will be fused together, and the six Chalices will be fused together. Ask when the fusion and sealing are complete; wait for this before going on.

13. Ask the Lords of Karma, Divine Director, the Karmic Board, your Dimensional and Interdimensional Archangels, and Archangel Metatron for the FULL REPROGRAMMING OF YOUR CRE-ATION TO FULLY ACTIVATE THE FUSION AND SEALING OF THE SWORDS, SHIELDS, AND CHALICES, AND THEREBY FULLY ACTIVATE AND SEAL THE INTERDIMENSIONAL PRO-TECTION OF YOUR UNION WITH YOUR GODDESS. Wait for this to complete.

14. Now ask the Lords of Karma, Divine Director, the Karmic Board, your Dimensional Archangel and Interdimensional Archangels, and Archangel Metatron for the FULL REPROGRAMMING OF YOUR CREATION TO MERGE AND FUSE, AND TO SEAL THE MERGING AND FUSION OF YOUR INTERDIMENSIONAL ARCHANGEL'S SWORDS, SHIELDS, AND CHALICES WITH THOSE OF YOUR DIMENSIONAL ARCHANGEL. Wait for this to be done; unless you receive a "no" response, it's happening. Ask when to go on.

15. Ask the Lords of Karma, Divine Director, the Karmic Board, your Dimensional and Interdimensional Archangels, and Archangel Metatron for the FULL REPROGRAMMING OF YOUR CREATION TO FULLY ACTIVATE THE FUSION AND SEALING OF THE COMBINED SWORDS, SHIELDS, AND CHALICES OF YOUR INTERDIMENSIONAL AND DIMENSIONAL ARCHANGELS, AND THEREBY FULLY ACTIVATE AND SEAL YOUR UNION WITH YOUR GODDESS. Request also to FULLY ACTIVATE AND SEAL THE TOTAL PROTECTION OF YOU, YOUR GODDESS, YOUR UNION, TOTAL UNION AND ASCENSION, AND ALL GALACTIC CORD SYSTEMS IN THEIR COMPLETELY SYN-CHRONIZED AND COMPLEMENTARY STATE. Ask for the complete insulation of your energy to protect the full activation and sealing. Wait for this to complete.

16. To finish, ask for these healings and reprogrammings in the name of the Light, on Earth and all other planets and between them, through all lifetimes and between them, through all dimensions, multidimensions and between them, of and between all dimensions of you and your Goddess's multidimensional Be-ing, union, total union, and ascension.

17. Ask for these things fully, completely, permanently, and forever, through all the levels and components of your Be-ing, all dimensions, all connections, all systems and between them, through all

multidimensions and between them of you, your Goddess, your union, total union, and ascension's multidimensional Be-ing.

18. Request these healings and reprogrammings immediately and instantly, past, present, and future, forever and NOW.

19. Thank the Lords of Karma, Divine Director, the Karmic Board, your Dimensional and Interdimensional Archangels, and Archangel Metatron.

Universal Healings

a) Repeat the full process above, but instead of doing it for *your* Creation and energy, do it for ALL CREATION AND ALL ENERGY.

b) Do the full process above, wording it for THE CREATION AND ENERGY OF YOUR GODDESS, AND OF YOUR GODDESS UNION.

c) Do the full process above, wording it for THE CREATION AND ENERGY OF ALL THE GODDESSES, GODDESS UNIONS, GREAT GODDESS UNIONS, AND ALL BE-INGS OF THE LIGHT.

d) Repeat the process again, wording it for THE CREATION AND ENERGY OF THE EARTH, THE SOLAR SYSTEM, THE GALAXY, THE UNIVERSE, THE COSMOS, ALL LIFE, ALL BE-INGS, AND ALL THE LIGHT.

e) Do the full process again, wording it for THE CREATION AND ENERGY OF ALL PLANETARY GRIDS AND STRUC-TURES, INCLUDING THE WELL OF LIFE AND THE FIRE OF LIFE AT THE CENTER OF THE EARTH AND ALL PLANETS, AND THE PLANETARY CORE.

f) Repeat the process once more, requesting THE REPRO-GRAMMING OF YOUR CREATION AND ENERGY TO INSTALL YOUR INTERDIMENSIONAL ARCHANGEL'S AND METATRON'S SWORD, SHIELD, AND CHALICE IN YOUR HOME, GARDEN, PETS, CHILDREN, AND CAR.

(Adults living in the home must make the requests for themselves.) Make sure the articles of interspace protection are all installed and are fully and forever activated.

These processes take twenty-four hours to complete, and you will feel it happening. You will not be closed up for them.

If you have been given permission to bring in a Goddess, have chosen and agreed to do so, and have done the work above, no more is needed at this time. All requests from here on are for you, your Goddess, your union, total union, and ascension. If you have not made them in this way for the processes of this book, you may need to repeat the processes. You will be told or know what needs healing in your Goddess. To do these healings for Her, make them as Short Process requests for you, your Goddess, your union, total union, and ascension, unless you are told to vary this. You will be guided as to what to do and what your Goddess needs, only follow the guidance of the Light.

First Quarter Moon in Taurus, March 28, 2001

Index